At the Park on the Edge of the Country

The Journal Charles B. Wheeler Poetry Prize

At the Park on the Edge of the Country

Poems

Austin Araujo

MAD CREEK BOOKS, AN IMPRINT OF
THE OHIO STATE UNIVERSITY PRESS
COLUMBUS

Copyright © 2025 by The Ohio State University.
All rights reserved.
Mad Creek Books, an imprint of The Ohio State University Press.

Library of Congress Cataloging-in-Publication Data
Names: Araujo, Austin, author.
Title: At the park on the edge of the country : poems / Austin Araujo.
Other titles: At the park on the edge of the country (Compilation)
Description: Columbus : Mad Creek Books, an imprint of The Ohio State University Press, 2025. | Series: The Journal, Charles B. Wheeler Poetry Prize | Summary: "A collection of poems about the legacies of immigration, Mexican American identity, pop culture, food, and ancestry from the perspective of a writer from Arkansas"— Provided by publisher.
Identifiers: LCCN 2024039854 | ISBN 9780814259368 (paperback) | ISBN 9780814283974 (ebook)
Subjects: LCGFT: Poetry.
Classification: LCC PS3601.R357 A8 2025 | DDC 811/.6—dc23/eng/20240909
LC record available at https://lccn.loc.gov/2024039854

Cover design by Brad Norr
Text design by Stuart Rodriguez
Type set in Adobe Caslon Pro

∞ The paper used in this publication meets the minimum requirements of the American National Standard for Information Sciences—Permanence of Paper for Printed Library Materials. ANSI Z39.48-1992.

Contents

I

Another Crossing *3*
Sight and Sound *4*
A Mexican American Novel *6*
My Documentary *7*
The Tostada *10*
Translation *12*
At the Park on the Edge of the Country *13*
Within Earshot of 1991 *14*
Lost Year *15*
At Lake Temescal *17*
Aperture *18*

II

The Bull *20*
Clearing *21*
Watching Him Cross *22*
After *23*
Someone Is the Water *24*
Debut *26*
Another Look *27*
Sancho Panza *28*
Betting the House *29*
At the Park on the Edge of the White River *35*
The Father *36*

III

Gathering *40*
Jamboree, Evening, Midsummer *41*
On the Road to Irapuato *42*
Irapuato *44*
Mexican in the Meadow *45*
Early Conversation with My American Grandmother *49*
Maintenance *50*
My Condition *52*
In Body Sweet *54*
Brothers *59*

Notes 61
Acknowledgments 63

I

Another Crossing

The river sloughs off mist, elk approach
its banks for a drink. Moon perched
in the mezzanine of the night. Dogs clamor
for each other miles away. I settle
onto this stone seat trying hard to see anything
but the men stepping into the rushing water,
each holding a small bag over his head. Striding
into the silence I've embraced. What crossings
can be made when already in Arkansas?
One of them falls hard into the White River,
foot probably catching on some rock's jag.
Those in front keep walking, those behind
go around his brief thrashing below the surface.
His mouth opens with ¡estoy bien!
when he rises, which disturbs the elk
who look up so that they might study him
with me, so that we all might behold the man
who is suddenly here, who, of course,
resembles my father, droplets tumbling
from his creased brow back into the current.
He blows snot from each nostril and runs
his fingers through the hair almost landing
on his shoulders as it does in my father's first photo
ID, taken in Mexico, listing the wrong birthday,
catching him as a teen, looking like this guy
hauling his hand across the surface of the water.
He works hard to match pace, impossible, like my dad
in the White River, crossing twenty-odd years
after the fact. Who needs dreams when I've got eyes.
The others emerge by the shore, disappear
into the woods, refuse to wait. The elk and me,
welcome committee. A stranger climbs into the bramble
where he hollers, gaining ground on the group.

Sight and Sound

Roxie Theater, San Francisco

I am led into the dark
cinema for a restored
print of a major work
by David Lynch
he speaks to us
in a previously recorded
introduction
every now and again
I try to turn my head
an imperceptible degree
to catch you in the glow
I am taking stock
of how I feel
suspicious
but of what
there's a woman
who makes occasional
smart comments
there's a man
eating chocolate
and popcorn
in fistfuls
your hand opens
for potential touching
holding your
perfume in my mouth
your leather skirt
squeaks in the seat
the sun's laboring
across the finish line
when we leave the theater
we walk toward

the bar where I'll lose
my wallet
in the film
a man with a powdered face
says hello at a party
in one of those big LA houses
he says hello on the phone too
he likes to watch people sleep
the main character
becomes someone else
driven by formless desires
I am afraid I am
alive I am turning
twenty-six today
at an auto shop
the young man
he has become is pulled
or manipulated between
the forces of duty
the forces of desire
cars are lifted hoods
popped some force
tells him come to
the desert I am still
pulling myself
apart when you order
cocktails I am still

A Mexican American Novel

The novel includes a protagonist with a mysterious scar slashed across his scrotum as well as numerous references to tax fraud, bruised fruits, and last names. A year-in-the-life type of tale. In a pivotal September scene, he asks his father whether anything weighs more than madness. (Readers will know the man's frown counts for an answer.) Then a flashback to when the father crushed his five-year-old son's fingers with a rising car window. A chapter entitled "Robert Hayden Was Rarely Wrong." The boy wanders from light source to light source: big moons, small lanterns, candles, burnt-out bulbs hanging on grocery store ceilings, and the various deep purples of a beloved's bedroom. I'm working out how he'll talk to lovers, but his legs will shake, bare but for goosebumps rising around his knees. In the first paragraph, the boy presses a guitar into a cloth case. By the end of the year, he'll understand what symbolizes great human suffering and what of the ordinary self remains.

My Documentary

I had a dream where the giant
brushes inside the drive-thru
car wash had been replaced
with the branches of pines.
My mother's car was scratched
to hell. When we left the wash,

there were children making
more men out of snow.
Once, I remember, my cousin,
who was around seven,
needed the restroom. I was fifteen.
We were waiting for our grandmother

to get off work. Why didn't
we just go inside? I walked him
to the edge of the parking lot,
near some pines that protected us
from the street. The lot was vacant.
My cousin began to pee and said, *Austin?*

I said, *Huh?* as he just went to town
all over my left shin, warm to my ankle,
soaking my sock, Nike Cortez. When
I came home, before I could change,
my father smelled it on me. He was furious.
He wanted me to beat my cousin senseless.

Didn't I have pride? I was
scared and, I hoped, stoic. I sat in the shower.
Another time, I was in the running
for a full ride in computer engineering.
The finalists stayed overnight
in the dorms with engineers-to-be.

I didn't ask my host about the difficulty
of coursework, if he felt any pressure
with the scope of the resources
he'd been given. I scrolled the online profiles
of the date I'd bailed on for the interview.
The next morning, I felt I was doing well.

There were four middle-aged professors
with their elbows on a wooden table.
My chair was situated in the middle
of the room. I think I blew it
when one of them asked me a softball
last question, the four of them smiling

in their light-blue button ups,
how would I describe my work ethic. I said
I worked like NBA 2K14, wherein I might
prioritize which skills to develop, etc.
While they shuffled their papers,
I acted as if I'd paused, comma,

to tell the story of a father, mine,
who migrated to this country
with ambitions so minor he managed
to accomplish them with his first paycheck.
This was mostly even true.
During my senior year in college, for a final

paper on Latino/a/x/e immigration to Arkansas
during the 1990s, I interviewed my father.
Time to get his border crossing down
in a way my speculative poems hadn't.
I felt—listening to him describe, backtrack,
revise, and reconsider the two times he crossed

the border, at fifteen and eighteen—
that *my life had sprouted from his life.*
This was, in most ways, a basic idea.
It was revelatory to me. The recording
and my notes are lost, but I remember details.
For instance, he traveled with men

whose last name was Araujo
but bore no relation to him. For instance,
when he reached Texas, he kept his feet
in Walmart bags instead of socks.
For instance, he said he swam for the first time ever
in the river separating one country from the other.

For instance, he considers the seed
of his decision to come to America
the time as a boy he watched a friend
greet his father who was home
from a season working fields in Alabama.
The man had a present with him.

It was a pair of Levi's jeans so new
they stained the boy's bottom, my father said.
He said he remembers, in Springdale,
a couple months before he met my mother,
how he blew a check on three pairs.
He bought them at Ryan's on Emma Street.

We'd shop for school clothes there. By the register
stood a life-size cardboard cutout
of Michael Jordan beside a measuring stick
where we could see how tall we weren't.

The Tostada

When I twist in my chair, I hear
my back crack like a fallen bag of tostadas.
Cabbage, sour cream, and hot sauce
were the toppings my mother preferred
on her tostadas when I was a boy. She didn't
grow up eating tostadas. The tostada
was something she learned to like. When I reach
into the plastic bag, the tostada cracks
at my finger's slightest touch like the first light
cracks open the dark. Today after his friend
told a good joke, I heard a man cracking up
on the street like a tostada that breathes.
The sidewalk cracked: the weather's tostada.
If you cracked open my skull, you'd find
me crumbling tostadas over the pozole
my mother would make on Christmas Eve
near midnight at a party. There's my parents
and there's my real life, I tell myself, chewing
on a tostada festooned with cabbage, sour cream,
and hot sauce in an autumn that, like many friends,
surprises me with its chill, here, in the west.
What cannot be said will be wept, said Sappho.
Tostadas are stale tortillas fried in oil
often topped with avocado, radish, and seafood
like shrimp, ceviche, or, I guess,
tuna. Tostadas from the supermarket come in plastic
bags, stacked like discs loaded with movies or music
to be distributed illegally. The excess bit of bag
gets tied up with a rubber band, little plastic ponytail
that could. My mother nibbles on a tostada
while she watches me gesticulate with nervousness,
pointing in several directions at once.
Where is your father, the therapist asked me
the other day. Oh, he lives

in Fayetteville, Arkansas. *No* (she smiled),
where in your life? With the tostada
I am breaking, or cracking open, my morning's fast.
This is the tostada speaking. In the dark,
the tostada lies on its back waiting to be cracked.

Translation

I can't get away
with speaking like this
on a daily basis. Only when
I remember what it was like
to be afraid long ago
in that first language
can I begin to know how it is
I cling to the earth now.

At the Park on the Edge of the Country

If you're wearing a tee one would call vintage nowadays
perhaps with a pop star or soda brand brandished
across the chest, waiting with your brother-in-law

for your brother at a bench in the park in which
you two will sleep, huddling together for warmth
and to shoo away thoughts of permanent disappearance,

you must be my father in Ciudad Acuña in 1991.
When the police shake you two awake, you will be
the boy wondering which direction to sprint

from fire. And where to place your hands when speaking
to someone with a gun. And how to come back for more.
If you dreamt of Kerrville, Texas, get another dream.

Within Earshot of 1991

The scene isn't too hard for me to imagine: a short
white girl with bright orange curls, "Little Red Corvette"
on cassette and blasting. Her car a metaphor
for a horse, a Mustang. She wears
a light green jacket that tells me
it's autumn in Arkansas.
If I turn around, I'd see her father emerge
by the driveway, making the walk from house
to barn, crossing the overgrown field
toward her as image gives way to theater.
Watch him arrive and shout at the girl,
making those noises that send her
inside herself. I can't quite make out his words—
like a movie a mother watches with the door
closed, leaving only the schematic of its voices
for her sons to parse. When he's finished,
he walks. In her car, she can control the music.
She pulls her jacket close, the chill of night
encroaching. A few birds flock to the shedding trees.
And somewhere under the machine
everyone and their mother calls a horse, a leak.

Lost Year

How tired I was of all that bunk
in the brain explaining how unfit

for everything I was. Then I came to a door,
a storefront from which music poured

into the street. There was a sign
saying come in and paint. I did.

I saw a spot at a table beside a man
who told me the goal of the group:

approximate the still life on the table.
I've been inept at visual arts since I was a child.

My mother would say
I don't know my own strength. The man

smelled of herb and offered me a puff
but I said I was waiting for someone

and wanted a clear head, a clean mouth.
His blond hair tied into a bun.

The woman in white coveralls beside him
did not raise her eyes from painting to say hello.

This endeared her to me.
Without looking, she asked

when I'd last heard a tree speak.
I didn't want to lie so I studied

a corner of the ceiling as if working hard
to remember. She said, yes, the ones around here

keep to themselves. She held
a large brush with her left hand, and the right

she kept behind her back as if to say en garde.
The still life comprised two vases,

green and orange, three apples, and a ball
of golden yarn. What brings you here, the man asked.

My friend told me it'd be fun,
they should be here soon, I said,

panning the room, but they were not there
on the couch or at any of the four tables

or near the locally made jewelry
the store sold during business hours.

At Lake Temescal

I'm sitting on a blanket not far from shore.
On days like this, my ankles,
before they brown, go red and sting.

A balding man throws a branch
into the lake. His dog wades beyond the line
of rope notched with orange plastic floats.

The border offers one definition of protection,
but the dog is prepared
to defy little rules like that.

It's not as though at the bottom of the lake
there are many sticks and many bodies of dogs.

By the time the dog has returned to him,
the man has moved on.
He picks out a beer from the cooler.

On the other side of the lake, people
fish on a dock, not moving much.

They expect something from the water—
it's not a new place to look.

Aperture

Made a mess
of my father's crossing.

In the dream, I delivered him.
If only to see him arrive,

if only in the dream.
That little kiss of a border.

But I couldn't write his name
on the fence. Even with paint.

II

The Bull

A lot of math went into my diet,
which I didn't care to understand.
I just ate until there was nothing left.
After that brief, joyous task

I had physical problems to manage.
If I didn't bite, kick, or charge too much,
no one would think I was mad
and I could continue standing,

sometimes paw at the floor.
When I was afraid, I ate.

My father seemed a stranger,
though I knew much about him.
He was also just a bull.

There were times he had been aggressive
then lazy like me. Neither of us could tell you
the color of grass. Of course,

I'm making my father up.
I saw another bull only once. When I died,
I'm told, some part of me retained at least a little use
even if most of me had to be thrown away.

Clearing

It was my mother not moving, not looking up,
that convinced me to root around the woods
near her house. The trees left.

She had no say over their demolition.
A neighbor inherited the plot,

needed room to build. His text read,
It's my birthright.

As boys, my brother and I would roam
to find a story in the dark.
There was that ancient shack

with dirty magazines, unused envelopes,
tins of dead gasoline.
Where everything married dust.
Back then I thought

I was going to explode with fright
and wouldn't step inside. I leaned
far into the frame, there was no door,

reaching out, touching the wooden floor,
lifting what debris I could
on the one side of that border.

You wouldn't have had to search hard to find us.
But I don't live there anymore.

Beyond the trees nearest my mother's house
there's now a clearing
and children chasing a dog.

Watching Him Cross

    What desire brims—so late in spring
this initial crossing. The river wants him still.

    My father stuck, scaling reeds. Mud anchoring
his boots. To pass time, he counts the stitches

    of his jeans. Maybe, he recites prayers aloud,
moves his lips, and whispers like he will to bless

    his children each night. Our arms, small allowances
of light, will be folded. Eyes closed, like his.

    He will not tell us of the cities along the way—
the story will start at the river, then, suddenly,

    Texas—when my chest begins to betray
me with cough, his hand will arrive honeyed

    with Vicks VapoRub—but not yet, but already
aching: now distant river: strawberry—

After

Tomatillos and serrano peppers
boiling in the pot—

I walk to the freezer,
reach for some ice.
The salsa will hurt.

My mother, at the table,
her hands bruised

from daily pricking,
accounts for her blood and its sugar.

She rubs one in the other,
over and over,
like she might heal it
with some heat.

Someone Is the Water

I am alone but for this vein
splitting the earth open
and we are silent, the stream and I

far away from our mouths. The stream
folds over itself, my hand
speculating under the surface.

The stippled faces of orioles
sail by slowly, their dark wings working
hard as tired men pulling oars

in a landscape painting, their lantern
chests dotting a modest pattern
across the sky, over this brook

a mile from your house—from you
who are alone but for your sons
and your sons' refusal to recognize

you cloaked under a sadness,
the color of whose cloth is muted
as these late-afternoon birds.

The stream sluices crawdads
and stones, carefully takes its bend
like a tongue spackled with canker sores.

I still expect it to speak. I've come
to listen to this slow
unfurling, hoping I'll fall

asleep as it turns like a lullaby
a child promises he will strain
to hear, to memorize. I make sense

of smudged pastoral visions.
Gone, the birds long gone.
Palms, I cup water with bent palms.

Debut

Stumbling, home for good that night, you wandered
into my bedroom and whispered my name.
I didn't respond. You took silence

as permission and sat on the edge of the bed.
Your face slipped out of your hands.

Through shadows I watched
your mouth move. Telling me a story.
We lost her, my eldest sister, when I was five.

Then your father followed, not two years later.
You asked if I remembered when we went to Mexico
and met their grave niches, high on a wall of marble.

I said nothing. But I did see their etched names,
which start with the same letter as my own,
so I heard the first vowel of an elegy
when you would call me to you.

You placed flowers into her vase, a Corona Familiar
onto his altar. I didn't reach across the silence.

I didn't break, my eyes nearly closed, acting asleep.

Another Look

Watching *The Thing* this weekend,
I decided to not look

away when I might usually,
which means I committed

my gaze on the men falling apart
onscreen. They do so literally

because of an alien parasite
and figuratively from paranoia
over who has and hasn't been

infected. A man is running
out of a building, snow

crunching underfoot. He doesn't
know if he's still himself.

Sancho Panza

When you sneeze, that means your lover's thinking of you.
You, swept up. The song of the breeze playing
in your hair. You, beneath the wind turbine and turn
of rotor blades. When you sneeze, my father would say,
that means your lover who is not your wife
is thinking of you. Rotor blades. Hair swept up
in that power. Beneath the power of a wind turbine,
in the hinterlands of northern Indiana, you,
me taking a photo. The car cooling off in the drift
of wheat where we do not belong. I raise
and peek through the viewfinder to capture
you beneath a turbine beside the highway
in the hinterlands of Indiana. On a common quest,
unfazed by delusions, swept beneath the power
of a turbine much taller than my father. The wheat
and the wind winding through it like speech,
like my father's voice, which is, remember,
in no way remarkable, unlike the originality
a sneeze summons, your face made new, your face
taken from you. On our way. Watching the wind
translated into energy for farms. In the photo,
you're sneezing, chronically, the wheat, the wind,
the sun, the drive, teasing your sinal
storm and rapture. My delusions? That I've got time
to admire your hair in the same wind generating power,
to take a photo, to ignore my filial obligations, to repeat
my silences, to extend seriousness to the wind, the wheat,
the blades slowly turning like the hands of the watch
ticking on my wrist. Because I am not who is on my side.
I am who I need to convince. I was born with doubts in me.

Betting the House

Once, I was sick and home from school
for the day. My father and I shared a shower,

steaming my seizing chest. And I, shivering,
noticed his legs for the first time,

daring then to study the hair lining them
and his arms, which too concerned me,

for they were darker than mine and muscled.
He palmed my brow, using the other hand

for the back of my neck, to keep me standing
under the full pressure of the water,

which was so hot I thought I'd lose my hair,
the heat loosening myself from myself.

He told me to hold my breath
but I got bored or began to strain,

and hid its release. After we dried
he warmed bowls of menudo,

and we ate and drank them on the couch,
in the first house my parents rented together,

a pink two-bedroom with a mulberry tree shading
the backyard, its fruit staining our limbs.

My mother and brother would stand side by side,
giggling at what they could paint

with the berry's juice, their faces sticky
with an ink not at all like blood, not at all

watercolor, but maroon as the menudo
I finished while I faded to sleep,

El Chavo del Ocho on TV.
Later, in a mortgaged home

in the Arkansas countryside, we were surrounded
by all types of birds, sighing branches,

bricks splitting apart where the moss
overtook them, surrounded by those nights

dragging the drunk of my father from the truck,
up the hill, into the house, onto bed.

And because our bodies will not last, I'm here
to forgive him for crossing into the night,

despite my coaxing, and my mom's coaxing,
and my brother's coaxing, despite his own once

and future departures, despite my final effort,
blocking the door with the full weight of me,

despite drifting in that moment between us,
of sizing each other up, in which we had to decide

whether to fall into more brutal discourse—
despite not stumbling into that fight,

which I surely would have lost, for my father, drunk
or not, shorter than me or not, would not have let

a pimpled and shy sixteen-year-old child touch him.
He went, truck keys in tow, wobbling along

from drink and coke. The project of loving him
won't end. This man who, when he came to Arkansas,

did not trade tequila for whiskey, did not begin
dipping snuff, leaving the brown juice in bottles

hidden in every room, did not
crawl into the thickets of a country

song looking for sorrow,
who would rather wake up each morning

recalling the silhouette of a lover's face,
who would rather know what I wrote

on the side of the paper lantern I loosed into the night,
the flame sashaying in the sky like the docked tail

of a dog, which vibrates instead of wags
while it licks the blood from my brother's ear,

smearing the dark pool across its mottled fur.
When my father was granted citizenship,

he wore a maroon polo and a thin goatee—
the hair serving only as an allusion to the two

bare patches of skin just below his bottom lip.
He barely smiles in the photograph of the judge and him,

taken, I think, by my mother, and his eyes don't tighten
in delight, his whole face blooms with surprise,

brow reaching back toward his hairline as if bolting
out the door behind the two of them standing

shoulder to shoulder, his lips parting slightly
as if about to speak. My parents printed the photo

for my brother and I to study after school, to understand
what becomes of the boy who crossed a river

with plastic bags covering his feet instead of shoes,
who slept in the park for days waiting

for his older brother to come back. But what happens now
to this man who disappears into the shadows to piss

while finishing another cigarette? What happens now that
the border patrol agent uses his fist to stamp the passport

and not the man's face when on his pilgrimage
to a mother who twirls her curls behind the ear

when nervous? What happens to the man now that
he's naturalized? While my father signed the paper, I sat

in a desk sneaking sips of Sprite in the second grade
at Robert E. Lee Elementary in Springdale, Arkansas,

where a concrete lion stood watch at the front door
baring green teeth. We, the children, would imagine

its flaking paint was its shedding scales.
We would say its ribs rose and fell.

We would swear the lion's toes curled
in the anguish of poor sleep. And one morning, my father

gripped a weed eater, slicing dandelions
and chipping rocks outside my bedroom

window, already far in his marathon of drink.
He'd come to reteach me how to work,

his blue, paisley-patterned bandanna
soaked, grass and flower petals

smudged along his forearms,
grease from the mower's oil staining

his fingers and knuckles, eyes
pooled with tears like storm runoff.

I donned basketball shorts, a gray tank top,
a pair of black Asics. All the while

he was listening to the never-solemn groove
of cumbia out of his truck's stereo, swaying

his hips and arms to the rhythm, the clear
articulation of the bass guitar thrumming

in my ear, the shimmer of accordion keys scoring
the green trimmer falling out of its spool. My father

swaying with the whacker the way he once twirled
his sister for the fifteen children crammed in the living room

who passed tamales and sopes around watching
them spin one another with a touch so light

they seemed to glide smoother than the song's
trombones. Who was he mowing the grass

while skunked for? What was he doing there at all?
After dusk had fallen, after my brother had come

from work to help me, after my father
had stopped dancing, after he let me quit

enabling his mystery
with maintenance, my brother and I lifted him

from his seat in the dirt to the cab of his truck
and we drove an hour to a motel.

Put him to rest. The drive home
scored with trap beat after trap beat.

Bet the house. Bet the yard.
The fence. The dog too.

Bury the dog, the father, and the younger son,
the older boy nowhere to be found.

At the Park on the Edge of the White River

My brother's breath stops when he sleeps—
his rest is not rest. In these hours
we've taken to talk, just the two of us,
he suffers beneath a filmy layer of exhaustion.
His eyes down, shoulders curving toward
each other. The boat of his brow
adrift in a pond of sweat. He perks up
to watch someone tubing downstream,
and I watch with him. We see this man drink,
glide, and disappear. We hear
two women walking on the path behind us,
their talking bright and trailing. Some sort of flower
grows on the cliff's border. A bird flies
overhead then skims the river. My quiet brother
glancing around. The thick black waves
of his beard a meadow at night
without any lightning bugs to clarify it.
I can't tell if he wants me to speak or not.
What I can read in his face are his eyes
studying something below both his chest
and his feet, a thing lower than this rubber
bench, in the dirt where he's let whatever
it is fall, and while I swear I had paid
such close attention to him, he surprises me
with what I miss in the midst
of my caring. It's his weeping.
It's my brother weeping.

The Father

Son, I hear you. My teaching was less than satisfactory.
You'd rather I'd taken you directly to the meadow

and pulled you into the grass, saying *this is a cattail,*
this is nameless, this is no good.

You didn't want to learn for yourself
what to remember.
One time, I heard you breathing

outside my bedroom door,
waiting for me to return
from a startless nap. That summer,
Arkansas put a blanket on me.

You know that. I speak your language.
Just like I know this country's story.
I passed the exam.

How could you describe me?
You haven't said what fruit I prefer.

Just from the record your voice has made
who would know what my wide nose looks like?

Or how dark my face is? How pretty.
That's fifty percent of me right there.

Let me tell you what. You'd think
I was anyone. An anonymous wetback.
I can say that. I'm average.

You? Mr. Iron Giant? Mr. Chacal
with your black-and-white mask
ready to trumpet me off the stage
for some errors, for some goddamn jokes?

You can't say anything without putting my name on it.

You're tall as heaven. You're so big
you made me doubt you were mine.
It makes me think God must be tiny.
That we must tower over our inventors.

I'm getting mixed up.
And you know all about being mixed.
Mixed feelings, cultures, languages.
There's not one thing clear about you.

I am the clearest thing about you.

What do I represent? The beginning?
Or the place you are headed?

Me, with all my flowerless faults,
all my vulnerabilities, helpfully
arranged and cataloged by you.

You want to separate yourself
from this great big turkey leg
of a nation? Is it not enough that at work
you sit and stare at computers in stalls,

saving you from burnt flesh,
from aching shifts in moonlight?
I hear the desks even rise and fall.

Maybe they always moved. I wouldn't know.
I've always been here, where you remember me,
in the factory, in the river, in your dreams.

Water of mine, when you travel,
when you are an outsider, on the run,
a mistake is how you get to know a place.

III

Gathering

There's a boy standing under a canopy,
arms cradled to catch what falls from the tree

or the gray throat of a sparrow. He hauls
the loot to a nearby stream so clear

the tadpoles in it shine like jewels.
He kneels close to them, face hovering

just above the folding surface,
lips moving, careful not to drink. His clasp

opens to offer a tadpole
what he has collected of fallen nuts, worms,

leaves, but the not-yet-frog
only billows and follows the current up,

perhaps to a fuller body like a river where
he pictures it might practice the art

of leaping with salmon, leaving this boy with his gift.
He extends again to the now-vacant water,

which keeps turning like a man
uncomfortable rising from bed

who clocks in at the packing plant
that dumps chicken shit into this stream

where his boy plays now, offering
dead things to a soon-to-be dead thing.

Jamboree, Evening, Midsummer

My hands, which kept my eyes safe
from the sun all day, now have little to do.
Fireworks in the festival sky, streamers
trailing a paper dragon's head. The phone

lights up with my brother's name.
Two boys run by me, colliding
and orbiting away with ease. A man, perhaps their father,

walks behind them and loses his fingers in their hair.
As I hold the phone to my ear, I stay trained on them,
the one boy looking up, the other staring ahead,
my brother's voice not yet breaking

their hold on me. But he's got some news.
The street's cut up into stalls for rigged games.
Temporary spotlights buzz.
Scent of coriander in the grass.

The boys are out of sight. At their age,
I'd pick goldenrod. I'd forget how to tie my shoes,
so I'd ask my brother. I'd hide
from our parents until he could help me.

On the Road to Irapuato

I wake carsick, my family singing
Juanes's "La camisa negra,"

and look up at el Cerro de Chipinque,
near Monterrey. We zoom along the highway.

Armadillos hide in potholes. Ahead,
men in mint bulletproof vests

have their knees on a man's neck and back,
his mouth so full of dirt

he could be a nursery pot.
My mother slows the car down

as we approach the checkpoint,
my father telling us again:

Don't be afraid, you're American citizens.
A soldier orders us to stop the car.

He escorts my father beyond
the checkpoint, asks him questions.

Another man speaks
to my mother. My brother and I don't

watch as they open our bags.
We worry for our PlayStation.

When they find nothing of interest,
a soldier waves his rifle.

My parents pile into the car,
which feels smaller now. My mother

drives. When we reach the hotel,
we take turns showering.

A man delivers us fried chicken.
My brother and I watch soccer.

The people on television gasp
at the precise aim of uniformed men.

Irapuato

Past the fountain of dancing water in Miguel Hidalgo Square, through a shop window, a fry cook grilled a burger, pressing the patty down sticky-note thin. My mother striding in and out of shops. She flashed a smile. My father bought my brother and me lucha libre toys with faces like melted butter. My brother ran between the market stalls. I chased. We had no answers for the butcher's questions. When she found us, my mother captured our relief with a shudder from the lens. She'd picked up a small plastic tray of strawberries. Smiling all day. Maybe this was what she dreamed of when my father convinced her of this trip. What she imagined when meeting him at the bar in Arkansas where the only words they could share with each other were *pizza* and *movie* and soon, *pregnant*. To the side of our portrait, elderly women were eating tacos with dragonflies and salt. I couldn't hear the crunch of wings.

Mexican in the Meadow

I watered a wilting succulent.
The sun had begun to disappear
behind the apartments across the street.
Afternoon turning quickly into evening.

In the oven, sweet potatoes roasted
on one rack, Brussels sprouts on the other.
Palo santo smoked on the sill.

Books with red spines spiraled like towers
or arms, like bricks or cells, around me.

I practiced my sigh in the silence, honing it
as one might sharpen a knife,
chest swelling then compressing
as my whistling breath left, returned.

Over and over as if breathing
required rehearsal,
the vegetables crisping,
filling the air with an earthy scent,

sigh after sigh hung in the room,
until they turned not into song,
as the voice might want,

but into sight, breath a manner
of seeing, a matter of looking.

There I was.
With the breathing.

In this mode, I looked around the room,
not the room of my boyhood,
where no one in my family sang.

And yet we filled the house with music:
guitars twanged there, radio often on.

Once, my mother gifted my father a harmonica.
I stared at the metal bar in his grip,
not knowing he would never put his lips on it,
would only rub it with his thumbs

as if to remove a film of dust,
revealing the actual owner's name
so he could give it up without having to play

before putting it back in the case,
setting that down, and walking into the cold
for a smoke with his coffee.

I didn't look for what might have been
happening in my mother's face,

what kind of sorrows might have dwelt there,
what behind her eyes could have been
glistening with the hoarfrost of sorrow,

its blizzard, its bite and information,
I would never know,
having chosen not to.

Look me in the eyes when I speak to you.
But it didn't matter what her child looked at.

Never mind the object of my gaze.
It was the direction of my looking
that would pull me out of myself.

After each of her surgeries,
a silence bore into these boys and this man
who felt something had been dangerously wagered.

These lost and losing ones escaped
when lonely to the nearby pasture
where they stomped on the uncollected straw
left by a neighbor's hired labor.

I placed, when lost like this,
stalks of hay in my hands, twirled them like pens.

I'd pick cuticles.
I'd chew hay.

Not looking would lead me to this field
where the horses refused to come close
to their fence. Not facing led me there

when I refused to look at her weeping
and moaning in the hospital bed

crying out for a relief more final
than the one it was possible to give her.
Her cry as if someone else's,
as if it could not be hers, my mother's.

I needed to place it,
tuck it under the mattress,
in the custodian's closet.

The cool of her eyes interrupted
with cracks of red
like the splayed veins
of a falling leaf,

the shake of her head in pain,
the tree losing those leaves
on the edge of a meadow not here.

Through the open window, a breeze
carrying the scent of honeysuckle.

And I, quiet, breathing slowly,
knuckles picked open.

Early Conversation with My American Grandmother

I kept saying jugo
jugo quiero jugo
stepping closer
to reach it myself
'til she grabbed a small
amber cup
from a cabinet
poured me some
I looked through the glass
of the sliding door
at two horses
in the field
I shouted for them
to run
come closer
but they just stood there
on all fours
doing nothing
not even eating

Maintenance

Walking up the hill after
    checking her mail, I see
        my mother has sat my brother

    in a plastic chair on the porch.
Outside it's simple to clean the mess

    of his buzzed hair,
        which might tickle her feet
    if shorn and swept
in the kitchen. She cradles

    his head in her hand,
        pulling him toward her.
    Her thin legs

upright, steady.
    The clippers hum and she
        holds them in her right hand

    as the left searches for the last
stretches of daylight.

    She pushes his skull.
        My brother's

    a young man staring
at the clothesline hung between
    two oaks.
        The wind lifts the twine

    of the line then pulls it down.
Down his head she slides

    the clippers, her slight
        arms raised, elbows
            bent and scabbed.
    When she trims

    the neckline, the machine
vanishes behind him
    and what's left

        of their touch
            for me to describe
        is her blue-eyed

    concentration and his
round brown lonesome face.

My Condition

A doctor came to visit me on some days.
She'd observe in the rattan chair beside the bed
where I was flat on my back

even though I didn't need the rest.
I wasn't sick, far as I could tell,
just completely ignorant.

She told me that my dream
had been to work as an actor.

Watch films, she said.
When you watch films,
you'll remember
that all a person is
is an image.

Of those she screened for me,
I liked the ones that didn't rely on color.

I didn't have the whole story down
but had no problem inventing many details

like the scholarly work
I'd neglected
before the accident
with its long digressions
on the epistemology
of hero worship.

The doctor, fingering the pockets
of her thin coat, didn't think much of that bit.
You did not forget your life by accident,

she said, *and you were no scholar,
but you could be a bit of a windbag.*

Then she touched my forehead.
When she left, I went for a walk.

I couldn't remember—
did I have many brothers

and sisters or had the whole
of the family's ambitions lain in my lap?

In Body Sweet

It happened that last June,
jogging down a street
in Indianapolis, my shirt
tight against my chest,
breath not turning over
quickly enough for my lungs,

I passed a table set just
outside a bar, full of men
in their fifties. One of them,
blue trucker hat on, shirt
black with orange flames
rising from the waist,

gave his friends the nod
watch this and asked me
I don't really remember
what, I invent it anew,
about my breasts, and
the feeling like a key turning

in the ignition, the shame
of a joke at my expense,
at this body turned joke,
made me for that moment
murderous, and the hole
in the floor of my mind

widened until I could look in
and glimpse the pint
of beer smashed against
this old man's mouth,
*see how you giggle with two
less teeth, I'll kill you,*

you, eating beside friends
who didn't quite laugh
when you said it, just smiled.
One I think nudged
stop the way we ask our boys
to quit, prey already dead,

outside of a sports bar
going out of business,
on the sidewalk tracing
Virginia Avenue in Fountain Square,
our gazes meeting for
the briefest as I jogged

past your group, having
not raised my voice
much less my fist, cowardice
or mercy, turning the options
over as I carried home
these breasts, which sprouted

as a boy. I remember,
so young, like eight,
goddamn, standing
in front of a mirror
alone in the bathroom,
while my folks watched

Sábado Gigante, as I clasped
my left breast
and pulled so hard
I yelped, pulled
as if I could tear it off,
and another night

I brought scissors
with me but I couldn't
bring myself
to pinch the blades together.
I worried for so long,
so early, no kidding,

about being mistaken
for a woman, enough
I would lean over tables
in school as if reeling
from a stomach cramp.
I hid myself

from the midsection
to the groin. Too, I was one
of those keeping
an oversized tee on while
swimming if at a public pool
and even once at Lake Wedington

during a summer barbeque
in which my father tended
thin strips of steak
on a communal grill,
having a sip from his beer
before giving the meat

a sip too, and to pass
the time before eating,
my brother and I started
for the water until
my mother noticed my
turning without peeling

and dismissed my vanity
with a swish of the wrist,
to throw her the shirt.
I walked, I think this is right,
to shore with my arms
around my chest until I reached

the shelter of the water,
submerging myself
with the solemn stage
presence of a pastor
dipping the reformed
supremacist into the river.

Which is what I was
really thinking on that run
home in June—it was as if
I'd been dunked into another
body, floating almost,
my knees keeping me

from falling down
the way a shark's fin
bobs in and out of water.
It was I, the reformed shark,
who came home that afternoon,
trudging into the bath,

reeking of a city in heat
and aborted exercise. Like this
I greeted my sweetheart,
who was decorating her toenails
a lacquered color so sweet
she had to paint my thumbnail too,

not touching my hand
but holding the brush steadily,
modeling sureness for me
in a way I know has many
antecedents and probably
is the opposite of radical love,

but it moved me enough
to catch myself admiring
my painted thumb while
I lotioned my legs for once.

Brothers

Not even my brother has joined me in the city.
His hours in the country include explaining
to day laborers much older than he is
how to use tools that may save their roof, fence, crop.

I know the paths around my apartment well.
I've come to a limited understanding of the trees.

But my brother is a voice. He sends me messages
at the end of his shift. Sometimes,
when he has no one watching him,
he will send me a question about basketball.

Our father comes from Mexico,
which, in our memory, was like what we imagined
Sicily to be: pastoral, nutritious,

with a strange government.
We talk about these things
when I visit him in the country.

I can never finish any work
when I reunite with my brother.
If he doesn't send me messages,
there's nothing for me to revise.

Notes

The Tostada: The phrase that begins "What cannot be said . . ." is popularly attributed to Sappho, but its true origins are contested.

The Bull: This poem is dedicated to Louise Glück.

Someone Is the Water: This poem is dedicated to my mother.

The Father: El Chacal refers to the character on the Mexican variety show *Sábado Gigante* who eliminated contestants during singing competitions by blowing into his trumpet. When I watched the show, in the early 2000s, eliminated contestants would be thrown "a los leones."

Early Conversation with My American Grandmother: The title riffs on William Carlos Williams's "The Last Words of My English Grandmother."

In Body Sweet: The title riffs on Gerald Stern's "In Beauty Bright." This poem is dedicated to Kendra Kay Wilson.

Acknowledgments

Thank you to the editors of the following journals for publishing some of the poems in this book, sometimes in earlier forms:

Adroit Journal: "Someone Is the Water"
Bennington Review: "Another Crossing"
Blood Orange Review: "A Mexican American Novel"
Borderlands: Texas Poetry Review: "Irapuato"
Gulf Coast: "The Tostada"
Memorious: "Gathering"
Missouri Review: "Betting the House"
Pleaides: "After"
Poetry: "In Body Sweet"
Quarterly West: "Sancho Panza"
The Rumpus: "On the Road to Irapuato," "Debut" (as "Genesis and a Lullaby"), "Aperture"
Salt Hill: "Maintenance"
Shenandoah: "Within Earshot of 1991," "At the Park on the Edge of the White River"
Southern Indiana Review: "The Bull," "My Documentary"
TriQuarterly: "At the Park on the Edge of the Country," "Mexican in the Meadow"

"Watching Him Cross" won the 2019 Vera Meyer Strube / Academy of American Poets Prize.

This book was made possible through the support, generosity, and attention of the creative writing program at Indiana University and the Wallace Stegner Fellowship at Stanford University. To my teachers, workshop mates, and students—thank you.

Shoutout to the enthusiastic efforts of Kristen Elias Rowley, Skyler Barnes, and the crews at Mad Creek Books / The Ohio State University Press and *The Journal* in the production of this book. Aimee Nezhukumatathil—it's an honor. Thank you for selecting my manuscript for the Charles B. Wheeler Prize and for your call in the middle of winter.

I am grateful to the people who helped to shape this book and shape me: Noah Davis, Alberto Sveum, Ajibola Tolase, janan alexandra, Adrian Matejka, El Williams III, Curtis Moneymaker, Jackson Holbert, Kiefer Ramsey, L. Renée, Jalen Eutsey, A. Van Jordan, Paul Tran, Cathy Bowman, Amaud Jamaul Johnson, Alison Thumel, DS Waldman, Molly Bess Rector, Stacey Lynn Brown, Dan "Sully" Sullivan, Geffrey Davis, Soleil Davíd, Patrick Phillips, Alex Sagona, S. J. Ghaus, Bernardo Wade, and Louise Glück. A huge-hearted thank you to Ross Gay for pointing me in the right direction, time and again.

And to Kendra Kay Wilson for reading and listening to these poems, for her conversation, and for urging me toward clarity. Thank you for designing your life with me in it.

This book is dedicated to my family, whose unwavering encouragement ensured its completion.

The Journal Charles B. Wheeler Poetry Prize

At the Park on the Edge of the Country
AUSTIN ARAUJO

Softly Undercover
HANAE JONAS

Sex Depression Animals
MAG GABBERT

Claim Tickets for Stolen People
QUINTIN COLLINS

a more perfect Union
TERI ELLEN CROSS DAVIS

Praying Naked
KATIE CONDON

Lethal Theater
SUSANNAH NEVISON

Radioapocrypha
BK FISCHER

June in Eden
ROSALIE MOFFETT

Somewhere in Space
TALVIKKI ANSEL

The River Won't Hold You
KARIN GOTTSHALL

Antidote
COREY VAN LANDINGHAM

Fair Copy
REBECCA HAZELTON

Blood Prism
EDWARD HAWORTH HOEPPNER

Men as Trees Walking
KEVIN HONOLD

American Husband
KARY WAYSON

Shadeland
ANDREW GRACE

Empire Burlesque
MARK SVENVOLD

Innocence
JEAN NORDHAUS

Autumn Road
BRIAN SWANN

Spot in the Dark
BETH GYLYS

Writing Letters for the Blind
GARY FINCKE

Mechanical Cluster
PATTY SEYBURN

Magical Thinking
JOSEPH DUEMER

Stone Sky Lifting
LIA PURPURA

Captivity Narrative
MARY ANN SAMYN

Blessings the Body Gave
WALT McDONALD

Anatomy, Errata
JUDITH HALL

Stones Don't Float: Poems Selected and New
JOHN HAAG

Crossing the Snow Bridge
FATIMA LIM-WILSON

The Creation
BRUCE BEASLEY

Night Thoughts and Henry Vaughan
DAVID YOUNG

History as a Second Language
DIONISIO D. MARTINEZ

Guests
TERESA CADER

Rooms, Which Were People
MARY CROSS

The Book of Winter
SUE OWEN

Life-list
ROBERT CORDING

Popular Culture
ALBERT GOLDBARTH

KILLING STELLA

I'm alone, Richard has taken the children to his mother's for the weekend and I've given the maid a few days off. Of course Richard invited me to come along, but only because he knew I'd say no. My presence would only have disturbed him and Annette. And I also wanted to be on my own at last.

I have two days ahead of me, two days to write down all that I need to write. But I've been struggling to collect my thoughts since that bird began singing in the linden tree. I wish I hadn't spotted it this morning. I owe it to my bad habit of spending hours by the window staring into the garden. If I had only glanced outside for a moment, it would never have caught my attention. Its plumage is the same greenish grey as the bark of the tree. I only noticed it after half an hour, because it began to screech and flutter. It's still so young that it can't fly, let alone catch insects.

At first I thought its mother would come back right away and take it back to the nest, but she's not returning. I've closed the window and I can still hear it screeching. But she's bound to come back and fetch it. She probably has other young to look after. Incidentally, it's screeching so loudly that she's bound to hear it if she's alive. It's ridiculous that I'm so unsettled by that tiny bird—a sign of the poor state of my nerves. My nerves have been in this pitiful state for several weeks now. I can't bear the slightest noise and sometimes, when I go shopping, my knees suddenly start trembling and I break out in a sweat. I feel it dripping down my breasts and thighs, cold and sticky, and I'm scared.

I'm not scared now, because nothing can happen to me in my room. And in any case they've all gone away. Except the glass of the window would need to be much thicker to keep me from hearing those screeches. If Wolfgang were here, he would try to save the bird, but of course he wouldn't know how to handle this situation any better than I do. We just have to wait, the mother bird will come back eventually. She has to come. I wish it with all my might.

Incidentally, nothing can happen to me in the street, either. Who in heaven's name would do anything to me? And even if I walked in front of a car, it wouldn't be bad, I mean, not really bad.

But then again I'm so careful. I always look left and right before crossing the road, out of habit: as I was taught to do when I was still a little girl. The only thing I'm afraid of is the empty space around me. You can't tell, though; no one has noticed yet.

She can't be further away than next door's garden, or the next one along from that. Every house here has a garden; ours is one of the biggest and untidiest. It's only there so that I can see it from the window. The leaves of the linden tree have finally appeared, since it's been so warm. Everything is several weeks late this year. Yes, it's seemed to me for some years that our climate is gradually shifting. Where are the blazing summers of my childhood, the snowy winters, and the hesitant, very slowly unfolding spring?

If it suddenly became cold again that would be very bad for the little bird. But I'm worrying unnecessarily, there's even a bit of a warm autumn wind blowing. It's not even as if that tiny bird matters so much, there are so many of them. If I hadn't seen and heard it, I wouldn't care.

And I didn't want to write about that unfortunate bird anyway, but about Stella. I have to write about her before I begin to forget her. Because I'll have to forget her if I want to resume my old peaceful life.

Because that's what I'd really like to do: live in peace, without fear or memory. It's enough for me to run my household as I did before, to care for the children and look out of the window into the garden. If one behaves calmly, I thought, one cannot get involved in other people's business. And I thought of Wolfgang. It was so nice having him around me every day. Should I have endangered our peaceful companionship over Stella?

No, things couldn't have ended worse for me if I had. Stella is avenging herself on me, and taking from me the only thing to which my heart still clings. But that's nonsense. Stella can't take her revenge, she was already so helpless when she was alive, how helpless she must be now. I am taking Stella's revenge on myself, that's the truth, and it's as it should be, however much I might try to resist.

Of course I've always known that the day would come, it didn't need Stella for that to happen. Sooner or later Wolfgang would have been lost to me. He's one of those people who has no illusions and accepts the consequences. I don't have any illusions either, but I live as if I did. I used to think I could start over again from the beginning, but it's much too late for that now, in fact it was always too late for that, except I didn't want to acknowledge it.

There could no longer be any point in anything, because Wolfgang moved away from me. And that's good for him.

I read somewhere that you can get used to anything, and habit is the strongest force in our lives. I don't believe it. It's only the excuse that we need to keep from thinking about the suffering of our fellow human beings, or indeed about our own suffering. It's only the excuse that we need to stop thinking about our own suffering. It's true, a human being can endure a lot, not only out of habit, but because a faint spark glimmers within them, which they secretly hope will one day allow them to break the habit. The fact that they usually can't, out of weakness and cowardice, does not speak against it. Or are there perhaps two kinds of people, those who get used to things and those who aren't able to? I can't believe that; it's probably just a matter of constitution. Once we reach a certain age, we are gripped by anxiety and try to fight against it in some way. We sense that we're in a hopeless position, and make desperate little attempts to escape.

If the first of these attempts is unsuccessful, as it generally is, we surrender until the next one, which will already be weaker, and which will leave us feeling still more miserable and defeated.

So Richard regularly drinks his red wine, chases after women and money, my friend Luise pursues young men who are young enough to be her son, and I stand at the window and stare into the garden. Stella, that stupid young person, escaped successfully on her first attempt.

I would much prefer it if I could switch places with her, if I didn't have to sit here and write her pitiful story, which is also my pitiful story. I would much prefer to be dead like her, and not have to hear the little bird crying. Why does no one protect me against its cry, against dead Stella and the agonizing red of the tulips on the chest of drawers? I don't like red flowers.

My color is blue. It gives me courage, and detaches everyone and everything from me. Richard thinks I only wear my blue clothes because they suit my face; he doesn't know that I wear them for protection. No one can hurt me when I'm wearing them. The blue keeps everything far away from me. Stella loved red and yellow, and it was in the red dress I gave her that she ran in front of a yellow painted truck.

That radiantly yellow death that hurtled towards her like a sun, I think it was beautiful and terrible like the death we know from the ancient legends.

I had to identify her. Her face was unharmed, but greenish-white and much smaller than it had seemed to me when she was alive. The disturbed and half-deranged expression of the last few days had fled from it, making way for an icy silence.

Stella had always been a little clumsy and shy, and even when she was cheerful, her regular, wide face was immobile. Then it blossomed from within to her lips. Stella had been very happy for a short time, but she was unable to learn the rules of the game, she couldn't adapt and she had to perish.

A frivolous and greedy mother had stuck her in a

boarding school as a child. I remember observing her then, about five years ago, in church. She knelt beside me, her face turned towards the monstrance, her eyes wide open, her lips arched slightly forwards, open and devoted. And with the same expression she later stared at the evening paper behind which Richard's face was hidden. Wolfgang saw it too. He blushed and grew pale, and finally he choked on something to distract my attention from Stella. At fifteen he knew just as well as I did what was happening in front of our eyes, and he was trying desperately to protect me from that knowledge, while my sole concern was keeping him out of the game, and so did exactly what I shouldn't have done, namely nothing.

While Stella, unable to conceal her single big emotion, slipped inexorably into her disaster and Richard tried to deceive us with his smooth bonhomie, I made an effort to remain oblivious to everything. For Wolfgang's sake and also for mine, because there's nothing I hate more than scenes and arguments, and even a tense atmosphere is enough to leave me disturbed and uneasy for weeks.

The loneliness and peace of my room, the view of

the garden, the tenderness that filled me at the sight of Wolfgang, was I supposed to put everything—and for me it is everything—at risk for the sake of a girl who ran dully and inexorably into her fate, condemned from the very beginning to be broken, with her simple, foolish emotion, by our disintegrating, divided world?

Well, it wasn't worth my trouble, but it should have been, because Stella's was the young life that I allowed to run headlong into a murderous metal machine.

One can perish in very different ways, out of stupidity just as easily as out of an excess of caution; the former seems more worthy to me, but it is not my way.

Luise, Stella's mother, didn't come until after the funeral. She'd been traveling, and nobody from her little provincial town knew where she had gone. By the time we were finally able to contact her it was all over. Richard had sorted it all out, well and appropriately, as he tends to sort everything out. Luise, and incidentally she had been with her boyfriend, a young postgrad student, in Italy, now sat facing us in our sitting room, sobbing.

Richard gave her platitudes, which sound more

convincing from his lips than from mine, words of genuine sympathy. His eyes were deep blue and moist, as they are when he is agitated or drunk, and I couldn't help thinking of the wreaths on the bare hill. There weren't many wreaths, by the way, because in this town Stella had only us and a few friends from school. I thought of the hill and of Stella's body, bled dry and crushed, in its wooden prison. For the first time I was filled with pity. It was foolish and absurd, because Stella was dead, and yet pity swelled within me like a physical pain that sat like a lump in my chest and radiated all the way to my fingers. And yet that pain was no longer meant for Stella, but for her dead body, which was now doomed to decay.

I heard Richard talking, but didn't understand any of what he was saying. Gripped with horror, I only saw his eyes, which were so moist and alive. Every hair of him was alive, his skin, his breath, his hands, and the sight of it took my breath away.

Seen from outside, we were a middle-aged couple trying to comfort a mother who was bent with pain. Except Luise is not a mother bent with pain. Stella's death was very timely for her. We knew that, and

Marlen Haushofer

KILLING STELLA

*translated from the German
by Shaun Whiteside*

A NEW DIRECTIONS PAPERBOOK ORIGINAL

Copyright © 2017 by Ullstein Buchverlage GmbH, Berlin
Translation copyright © 2025 by Shaun Whiteside

All rights reserved
Except for brief passages quoted in a newspaper, magazine, radio, television,
or website review, no part of this book may be reproduced in any form or by
any means, electronic or mechanical, including photocopying and recording,
or by any information storage and retrieval system, or be used to train generative
artificial intelligence (AI) technologies or develop machine-learning language
models, without permission in writing from the Publisher

First published in 1985 by Claassen Verlag. Published in 2017 as *Wir töten Stella*
by Ullstein Taschenbuch Verlag

Published with the support of
≋ Federal Ministry
  Housing, Arts, Culture,
  Media and Sport
  Republic of Austria

First published as New Directions Paperbook 1641 in 2025
Manufactured in the United States of America

Library of Congress Cataloging-in-Publication Data
Names: Haushofer, Marlen, 1920–1970 author | Whiteside, Shaun translator
Title: Killing Stella / Marlen Haushofer ; translated from the German
by Shaun Whiteside.
Other titles: Wir töten Stella. English
Description: New York : New Directions Publishing Corporation, 2025.
Identifiers: LCCN 2025016291 | ISBN 9780811238656 paperback |
ISBN 9780811239578 ebook
Subjects: LCGFT: Horror fiction | Domestic fiction | Novels
Classification: LCC PT2617.A425 W513 2025 | DDC 832/.914—dc23/eng/20250407
LC record available at https://lccn.loc.gov/2025016291

10 9 8 7 6 5 4 3 2

New Directions Books are published for James Laughlin
by New Directions Publishing Corporation
80 Eighth Avenue, New York 10011

she knew we knew, but she sobbed and wept as her role demanded.

Now that Stella's legacy, the pharmacy, has come to her, Luise can marry her postgrad, who would never have taken her without the dowry. She can buy this strong young man and persuade herself for a while that she was lucky.

Stella had become a burden to us all, an obstacle that had finally been cleared out of the way. Of course it would have been even better if she'd had a happy marriage, emigrated, or otherwise somehow disappeared from our field of vision. But she had disappeared at any rate, and we were able to forget her for once and for all.

I could tell by looking at Richard just how much he'd forgotten her already, since for him forgetting is a physical thing. His body has already forgotten Stella; tall, broad, and hungry for new women and new sensations, he sat next to me and patted Luise's thin bird fingers with his broad well-tended hand, which is always dry, warm, and pleasant to the touch.

And Luise's whimpering fell silent under that warmth, under the sound of his calming voice.

"I always told her," she groaned, "pay attention when you're crossing the road. I would just like to know what she was thinking of."

"Yes," Richard said sorrowfully, "we would like to know that too, wouldn't we, Anna?"

He looked at me and I nodded. There wasn't even a hint of irony in his voice. I apologized and said that I needed to check on the kitchen. I didn't go into the kitchen, however, but into the bathroom and started putting on a bit of rouge. Pallor doesn't suit me.

Stella had been pale in the last few weeks too, but she was nineteen, and suffering refined her face, making it more adult and charming. A woman over thirty needs to be able to stop suffering, it doesn't do anything good to her appearance by then.

When Stella came to us, her skin was slightly tanned. She was beautiful, but lacking in charm and grace. She was a bit too healthy and strong for modern tastes. Indeed, it later took a heavy truck to crush the life out of her body. It was so considerate of Stella to make the whole thing look like an accident. And it showed how little Luise had known her daughter that she believed she had stepped off the curb unintentionally. Because Stella's dreaminess was that of a sleepy, strong, young animal finding its way through the bustle of the city as if in a trance. Not even the driver of the truck, a simple, ignorant young man, believed it was an accident. Stella wanted to die, and with the same unreflective self-abandonment with which she had once dropped into life, she fell out of the same life that had neglected to hold on to her with a bit of love, kindness, and patience. We have cause for gratitude. How embarrassing it would have been had she taken sleeping pills or thrown herself out of a window. Her elegance, which was an elegance of the heart, showed itself in the manner of her death, giving us all the opportunity to believe in a meaningless accident.

But what use is all of this if the only person who should really have believed it does not believe it and never will? Stella will always stand between me and Wolfgang. The time of childish tenderness and trust has passed. Wolfgang abhors his father and despises me for my cowardice. He will only understand me much later, when he goes from one room to the other as I do, alone with my unease and the knowledge that the prison is completely inescapable. But by then I will have ceased to be, just like my father, whose ironic laissez-faire attitude filled me with insecurity as a child. The eye that fell upon me when I played with my dolls is the eye with which I follow Wolfgang when he goes to play tennis with his friend, and with which he already observes his little sister's games.

If Wolfgang were with me now, he would try to save the bird in the linden tree, and I would need to deter him, because if the mother bird doesn't return the little one will be beyond help, it can't eat on its own. Only its mother could save it, and I'm starting to doubt that she's coming back. It has grown smaller than it was, I'm sure of it, even though it was already so tiny in the morning that I couldn't imagine a smaller bird. I can see it clearly now, a little bundle of feathers opening its beak and its eyes wide with fear and hunger. Its mother isn't going to come. I've closed the window again. The sun is shining on the little bird now. Maybe it will go to sleep and I'll have a few hours of peace if I know it's safe. All this crying is draining its strength away far too soon. Perhaps it's thirsty, in fact it must be. But how ridiculous to be bothered by a bird. Richard would laugh at me. I just have to believe that its mother will find it. Sometimes I find myself thinking that it's my inability to believe that attracts calamity. Perhaps Richard would never have become the person he is today if I had blindly believed him, perhaps everything would have been different if my father had not looked at us so strangely the day I brought Richard home. How could he have known, who gave him the right to know what was to come, and who gives me the right to pursue Wolfgang with my eyes just as I pursued Richard and Stella?

We need to get used to looking past people and things, we should never allow our thoughts to deceive us. It would be even better, of course, if we could stop thinking, because even our thoughts kill. I thought: "He will destroy Stella." I thought it for long enough for it to happen in reality. I know that Richard is afraid of my thoughts. Superstitious, like everyone with an energetic constitution, he fears only what he cannot grasp and understand for himself. But he is strong enough to push that fear aside, as he pushes aside everything that would get in the way of his plans.

Why did nothing warn me on that September evening, when Stella came to us? Why didn't I simply turn down Luise's request? It didn't suit me at all to take this strange young woman into our home, and even Richard wasn't exactly thrilled with the idea. He only agreed for my sake and because Stella was only supposed to stay for ten months. Luise is my friend, that is to say she has claimed to be my friend for thirty years. I've never liked her, not even at school, because even as a child she was stingy, duplicitous, and hateful. Luise always wanted to have my things, in those early days she stole my erasers, patent leather belts, and sausage sandwiches, later she wanted the men who wooed me, and now at last, with the help of her daughter, she has destroyed the peace I'd struggled so hard to find. She is a bringer of misfortune, Luise, ugly, dried-up, and boy crazy. But I've never managed to persuade Richard that she's just a burden to me. He simply doesn't understand that there are some people you despise and still cannot escape. Never in his life would Richard have found himself in such a situation. He shrugs off everyone who isn't of use to him in some way or other. Even Stella wasn't much use to him for long; a few weeks, nothing more. She made him far too uncomfortable. What could a seducer like him do with this clumsy, earnest child? No woman has ever bored him as quickly as Stella did.

Richard had never seen her before. Luise always tended to travel without her daughter, and he had formed a quite mistaken impression of Stella. Even today I can't believe that Stella was really Luise's daughter, even though there can be no doubt about it. Stella's father must have been an irresponsible fellow if he managed to spawn a child with Luise. He seems to have immediately regretted this development and tried, by drawing up a will that was as refined as it was shortsighted, to protect his child from his wife by making Luise the beneficiary of his financial assets while Stella would inherit the pharmacy. But he really shouldn't have arranged his will like this, because as a result he created an *implacable* enemy for his daughter. The best thing that Luise ever did for Stella was to put the child—who was often terrified, crouched in a corner at home, becoming more and more of a hindrance—in a convent. There, Stella found so much love that she was able to store it up and live off it for eight years. Of course she really should have studied pharmacy, but that training was not what Luise had in mind—the less Stella understood of what she was supposed to understand, the better it was for Luise. But since Stella had to do something, in the end, and her mother had no use for her whatsoever alongside her women friends, dogs, and lovers, she hit upon the idea of foisting Stella off on me, at least for a year, or as long as her business studies course lasted. In quiet despair, Luise must've said to herself that the day of Stella's maturity was drawing ever closer. That wouldn't have been her downfall, of course, because she still had a legacy, and she had certainly become rich enough over the past few years, barely hampered by an old and half-demented guardian. But then again there was also the matter of this young man whom she was determined to marry, but whom, as she was probably well aware, she could only *buy*. It was a hopeless situation for her, I admit.

So Stella came to us, pushed aside once again by her mother, and also not eagerly awaited by us.

Our household, in fact, is set up in such a way that

it cannot withstand an intruder, or even a guest. For reasons that are only too obvious. Richard's friends will never be my friends, and Richard finds my friends uncongenial. Apart from this, no one else is familiar with the countless taboos that we must observe in our dealings with one another, and which must be respected even by the children. Consequently, our topics of conversation are somewhat restricted, but of course that's better than ceaseless friction. Then there's also the fact that a stranger would destroy my relationship with Wolfgang: everyone disturbed the two of us in those days, even little Annette, and of course Richard too. For that reason I didn't take on a maid as such, but a *cleaner*, a morose and sulky person who has no interest in us, we are nothing more to her than the people whose floors she cleans in return for a decent wage. She simply does her work, entirely governed by ideas and worries about people that we don't know or care to meet. People on the moon couldn't be any stranger than we are to her. Even though it's never mentioned, there were two sides in our house: Richard and Annette—Wolfgang and me, and we adhered strictly to the rules of the game. Richard had brief and slightly too cordial conversations with his son, to which Wolfgang responded with perfect politeness, and Annette would sometimes sit on my lap, and of course I put her to bed and she would kiss and hug me. But that isn't entirely true. I think Wolfgang has always loved his father, even though he sees straight through him, and if there is a secret pain in Richard's life, its name is Wolfgang. His son's otherness must cause him suffering, if Richard allows himself to suffer, because in fact Richard is seeking a friend, and Wolfgang will never be his friend. Where little Annette is concerned, I would probably love her instinctively if she weren't so much like her father. It isn't her fault that the very sight of her sometimes fills me with horror. I see her blossoming little face, I feel her warmth and hear her laughter, and know that they mean just as little as Richard's warmth and laughter. Both of them, Annette and her father, are born decoys, traps that God, or whoever, has set for other people, the heavy, loyal, imaginative, and emotional ones. Perhaps Annette is also too healthy and happy to be truly loved. This child will always achieve what she wishes for, and will never wish for anything unattainable. She is just as weak and helpless as a young tiger or a carnivorous plant. Richard is proud of this daughter, but basically he knows exactly who she is: a good-natured companion as long as he indulges all of her moods.

But since he has never loved anything as much as himself, he must also love this little image of himself.

Sometimes he gives Annette a mighty slap, which she takes with a quiet whimper. He has never struck Wolfgang, who is one of those children that one doesn't strike. Richard is much too clever to show weakness and put himself in the wrong.

During her first weeks with us, Stella was a terrible bother to all of us. Richard, who loved drinking his red wine, smoking and reading in the evening, suddenly felt forced to make conversation with a girl like Stella and found it terribly tiring and utterly pointless. Annette was simply jealous, as she is of anyone who lays claim to the interest of those around her. Wolfgang felt disturbed by the change in atmosphere, and I had a sense of being too quiet and not knowing how to deal with young girls. It seemed impossible to guess Stella's thoughts and respond to them. This tall, pretty, slightly too well-built girl was an alien element in our house, and she must certainly have felt that herself. She was more timid than shy, inhibited by her years of life in the convent, and I thought she must have seemed a little strange there too. She wasn't at all cute, childish, and silly as young girls tend to be. In fact she looked like a woman who is only still a child by chance. And as quiet as she was, it was impossible to ignore her. The dreadful brown clothes that Luise had bought for her were unbecoming enough, but she could not simply be ignored.

I had tried to adapt the spare room in which Stella was expected to live to the needs of its young new resident, arranging a few knickknacks around the place, the kind that young girls like, and covering the dark furniture with lace doilies. Then, when I actually saw Stella, I wished I could have cleared all of those odds and ends away, but by then she had already seen them, which meant that it was no longer possible. So the horses, dogs, and ballerinas stayed on the chest of drawers and looked quite strange beside this tall, earnest girl. I imagine that Stella never really studied. She sat in front of her exercise books and her textbooks and was simply bored. She was bad at math, and probably the slowest of her class at shorthand. In fact I had no idea if she had any real talents or skills. She was good with animals and plants, she liked doing menial work, and knitted jackets and socks from coarse gray wool for some poor people or other. Then she sent those rather shapeless things to her old convent. Richard like to tease her about her charity work. Then she would open her wide, white eyelids and laugh quietly and clumsily, like someone who has yet to learn how to laugh. She only knitted them to avoid accusations of laziness, and so that she could spend hours alone with her thoughts.

I knew nothing at all about those thoughts. Sometimes I doubted that she was thinking anything at all, her face was so still. She liked engaging with Annette, and the child finally began to return her affection. At first Wolfgang observed her with a mixture of curiosity, shyness, and prejudice. In that too he was every inch my son; it would never have occurred to him to approach a stranger. When it became clear to me that I would never be able to have a real relationship with Stella, I began to abandon my efforts and went back to living as I had done before, as if there were no young girl in my spare room. She still disturbed me, but I knew that the disturbance would not last for very long. I was always friendly toward Stella, just as friendly as I am with my cleaner, the mailman, or Wolfgang's friends from school.

I started yielding to my own thoughts again, walking from one window to another, smoking or with my hands pushed into my sleeves, gazing into the now bare garden. I bought flowers, which became increasingly expensive as the cold season progressed, I dutifully went for walks with Annette, and I talked to Wolfgang about the books that he was constantly devouring, some of which were perhaps unsuitable for him. Of course I also took care of the housework, got annoyed with Annette, who was lazy and slovenly at school, and, as usual, discussed with Richard all sorts of matters relating to the children and the housekeeping. I did everything according to routine; for me reality meant staring into the garden, wandering restlessly around the house, and feeling warmth in my breast at the sight of Wolfgang.

Something had happened to me years ago that left me in a diminished state, an automaton that just gets on with its work, barely suffers, and is only turned back for seconds at a time into the living young woman that it once was. The touching curve of Wolfgang's neck, the roses in the white vase, a draught billowing the curtains, and all of a sudden I'm aware that I'm still alive.

Then there's the other thing, which fills me with fear, with horror, with the feeling that something's going to jump out at me at any moment and break down the invisible wall.

I know that can't happen, but it forces its way into my mind, time after time, staring at me from the faces of strangers in the street, rising in the howl of a dog, filling my nostrils in the butcher's shop with the stench of blood, and touching me like a cold hand at the sight of Richard's full, cheerful face.

Something must have happened to me years ago; since then I don't think I've been able to tolerate the idea that, incomprehensibly to my brain and heart, good and evil are one. To be able to endure that knowledge, one would need the vital force of a giant. But giants do not find themselves in this situation; for them, thinking is replaced by a sturdy cudgel. They prefer to live. Thinking people must always give up living, and living people do not need to think. The act of salvation is never performed, because anyone with the strength to carry it out is unaware that they must do it, and the knowing person is incapable of action

Stella was one of the living. More than a person, she was like a big gray cat or a young deciduous tree. She sat at our table, thoughtless and innocent, waiting for fate. Richard would have needed only to reach out a hand to grip her tanned wrist. He didn't, but he smiled as he cut up the meat on his plate, calmly, relishing each movement.

Richard is a born traitor. Equipped with a body that grants him constant pleasure, he could live contentedly, were he not gifted with a dazzling intelligence. It's this intelligence that turns the pleasures of his sensual body into crimes. Richard is a monster: a considerate paterfamilias, a valued lawyer, a passionate lover, traitor, liar, and murderer.

I have known all this for years, and if I knew who I could hold responsible for this knowledge, I would kill them. I used to see only guilt in Richard, and I began to hate him. But now I have known for a long time that he is not to blame if I react like this to the fact of his presence. There are so many others like him, the whole world plainly knows and accepts it, and no one puts him on trial. Whose fault is it that I can't just accept things as they are? I am slowly giving up hope that someone, I don't know who, will one day take a stand, and even if they did, I wouldn't know how to respond. My rage went up in smoke long ago; all that remains is the horror that dominates me completely, and that I inhabit, in which I am trapped. It has entered me, it has saturated me, and it accompanies me wherever I go. There is no escape. My worst thought is that even death could not be deadly enough to extinguish it at last.

But horror and the knowledge of the truth that one is not supposed to know belong to the order of everyday life. Yes, I cling to this order, to the regular mealtimes, the work that returns every day, the visits and walks. I love that order, which allows me to live.

One day I was struck by the touching equanimity with which Stella wore her clothes, those brown, claret, and purple horrors that were either too big or too small for her, and which testified to Luise's wickedness. "We should buy her decent clothes," I said to Richard, "and she would be a beauty." He glanced up from the newspaper, gave me a surprised look and said, "Do you think so?"

I know his weakness for delicate, distinctive women. I went on to praise Stella's merits. He laughed and rocked his head regretfully back and forth: buying clothes for her was none of our business. In two years, once she was in possession of the pharmacy, she would start dressing decently. "Luise," I said, "is a disgrace." Richard raised his shoulders comically, shook himself a little and laughed. Suddenly I had an idea. What if I taught Stella how to dress? I closed my eyes and saw her coming down a flight of stairs in a white dress, smiling with her lips in a Cupid's bow, her reddish-brown hair shiny and loose, young, beautiful and seductive. I saw Richard's white, firm hands holding the newspaper, and was filled with a kind of satisfaction that he couldn't see this beauty, obstructed as it was by his penchant for an artificial, refined prettiness.

Over the following weeks the seamstress came to the house and sewed a few dresses for Stella, out of cheap materials, but in bright colors suitable for a young girl.

The transformation was complete. Stella stood in front of the mirror and saw herself as what she really was for the first time. "You're beautiful, Stella," I said, straightening a crease. She didn't look at me, and spoke seriously into the mirror, "I'm beautiful," amazed, surprised and finally overwhelmed by the new feeling that my words and her reflection had awoken in her, and then said again, "I'm beautiful."

Now I could actually have triumphed. Luise, the dragon, had been outwitted. It was entirely possible that the newly transformed Stella could bring home a fiancé who would ensure that in the future Stella's fortune would not be turned into Luise's clothes, hats, and lovers. But strangely I was unable to rejoice in this idea. Incidentally, I have never been gratified by a triumph, it usually makes me embarrassed, or puts me in a slightly painful state of mourning. Perhaps it's because my triumph means the defeat of someone else; I transform myself into that other person and suffer on their behalf. Luise, however, was so repulsive to me that I couldn't summon that feeling for her. What troubled me in my joy was Stella's face in the mirror, that gleaming face, that young, blossoming flesh, and that gaze devoted entirely to her new brilliance. I felt a creeping unease. Stella was no longer the child that she had been. There was a void in her breast, and it would draw the world toward it. And I didn't like that. It was not within my power to guide the flow that would fill that void. "Stella," I said quickly, "Stella, shouldn't you practice your shorthand today?"

She covered her eyes with her hands in a touchingly childlike gesture and turned toward me. Her arms fell to her sides, the gleam in her eyes was extinguished, and she turned toward the door with a sigh.

That evening Richard hadn't noticed that a new Stella was sitting across from him. But Annette noticed it and so did Wolfgang, who gave me a thoughtful, quizzical look.

Stella, in her strawberry-colored dress, ate hardly anything and stared dreamily into the distance. Fully in command of her healthy young body, she absentmindedly took little sips of her tea.

The bird is still sitting in the linden tree. It hasn't

stirred from the spot all night. It isn't screaming any more, just cheeping faintly. If I close the window, I can't hear it anymore. It's so tiny now that it can barely be called a bird. Its mother hasn't come, and I don't think she's going to.

When I'm alone in the house I'm always aware that this isn't my house. Sometimes I feel like a lodger here. All that belongs to me is the view of the garden, nothing else. Once I imagined that I would at least have something I could call a home, but since Stella's death, the gilded cage has turned into a dungeon. If I'm not mistaken, the garden has even moved further away from the house. It's moving away from me, slowly, almost imperceptibly, one day it will disappear completely, and I will stare out of the window into the void and think, that's where the linden tree used to be, and over there the patch of lawn with the viburnum bushes. Perhaps this has something to do with the windows. They are gradually becoming more opaque until they will finally obstruct my view.

Outside, it has started to rain, that's good for the bird, as long as the rain isn't cold. The rain will refresh it a little, it must be parched. I don't think it's suffering very much. Its weakness will doubtless be making it dull and sleepy. It has fallen from its world, from the hand of the bird god: I can't help it, and must try to forget about it.

But I want to write about Stella, and about how we killed her.

It began with the accursed new dresses—no, not with the dresses, it began with me inviting her into my house. I should have known that Richard would never respect any boundaries, that he doesn't respect anything, and that a big, simple child can be a very charming change for a man who is sated with every kind of love. You can't bring the lamb into the wolf's cage, and that's exactly what I did. I wonder why that torments me so much. To whom am I accountable, and whose punishment should I fear? I know that I am not pursued by moral or ethical considerations. I think each person is governed by their own laws, and they have boundaries drawn for them that they can't cross without destroying themselves. My law was the unimpeachability of life, and I crossed my boundary by calmly and thoughtlessly allowing Stella's life to be destroyed in front of my own eyes.

It's not my intention to accuse Richard. My task would have been to nurture life and protect it against murderous attacks. And what have I actually done? I've led the life of a woman in good circumstances, leaned against the window, and inhaled the scent of the seasons, while all the time I was surrounded by killing and injury.

I shouldn't be surprised if the garden is beginning to repel me. The mysterious force that makes the leaves of the linden tree turn green was the same force that drove the blood through Stella's young body, that gentle, red sap that ended up lying in great pools on the cobblestones.

The linden tree knows about my betrayal, and the dying bird knows it too. They don't want me any longer. I read it in the eyes of the children, I sense it when I stroke strange dogs and cats, and when I feed the hyacinth on my little table, it freezes in fear and self-defense. Traitors aren't forgiven, its shining flowers tell me, and its fragrance reminds me of the sickly smell that rose from Stella's coffin.

Of course I could continue running away from the knowledge, but I've had enough of running away. I know that admitting my guilt won't make anything better. It won't even come as a relief to me. I've never understood the benefit of confession. It may exist for other people, and I hope it does, but the powers to which I am subjected do not forgive and forget. They repudiate the insubordinate child forever.

I remember once cutting tiny peony buds from the already faded bushes. I had hoped I could keep them alive for a few days, and the next day they actually started opening. The little petals extended before my eyes, and then the terrible thing happened: as if their dead mother's green hands had suddenly let go of them, they fell on the tablecloth like little pink balls.

That's also how the big green hand from which I came let me go. I fall and fall, and no one will catch me.

Stella, still loved in the damp earth, and held by a hundred little root fingers, how much more definitively dead am I than you!

Two months after Stella came to us, I saw for the first time in Richard's eyes the alert, appraising expression with which he tends to pursue women. He'd probably looked at Stella like that before, and I just hadn't noticed. No one is more easily deceived than

I am. I get bored when I'm supposed to involve myself in other people's affairs—I find it repellent to the depths of my soul.

Back then, in mid-November, I was entirely preoccupied with Wolfgang. We were translating the *Iliad* together, and the sight of Wolfgang's eager young face made me as calm and relaxed as a person like me can be. I know it wasn't happiness, it was something quite different, a substitute happiness for people who have for some reason renounced the real kind. My room was our little ship, and while we stood before Troy, reality fell around us. Achilles, Wolfgang claimed, had simply been hysterical. He wrinkled his nose disapprovingly, and I understood him all too well, even though I have always regretted the fact that the beautiful madness of the ancients has been so wretchedly misunderstood and diagnosed as hysteria in our own time. Wolfgang, of course, wouldn't have been able to guess that in the not too distant future our cheap hysteria would turn once more into beautiful madness.

Back then his heart was beating for Cassandra, to my great admiration, since I didn't think she was an attractive figure for a young boy. But why, in fact, should he not have sensed that she is the true hero? Why do we underestimate our children so much? A little while ago I came across one of my old school essays and was lost in admiration. I couldn't remember writing it. But I recognized the familiar childish handwriting, the hand of a credulous, unbroken fourteen-year-old. What had become of her in the years that followed? I don't know, and as I stared at the page I was filled with envy and admiration—I, a forty-year-old woman—with the certainty of a great loss in my heart.

Sometimes Wolfgang says something brilliant. He will do so less and less frequently with each passing year, and in the end he will stand by a window like me, filled with dull grief over things half-forgotten and never known. A tall man, somewhat too gaunt, with thoughtful gray eyes and nervous hands, lighting one cigarette after another and stubbing them out, helpless as I am, as my father was, and that remote ancestor who was the first to sense the ticking of unease and stepped to the window of his cottage.

So then, in November, when I was so busy with the *Iliad* and Wolfgang, one evening Stella told me that she was going to take Italian classes, and that she wouldn't be home until nine o'clock three times a week. I looked at her, standing in front of me, a delicate blush on her slightly too-high cheekbones, her long fingers intertwined, avoiding my eye. I didn't think she'd ever be able to learn Italian, because she had no gift for languages whatsoever, but her intention was certainly praiseworthy. Also I didn't care either way, as far as I was concerned she could learn Kirghiz, which would have suited her much better, by the way. Stella wasn't my child, she was free to do as she pleased. I said something about cold suppers and plunged back into the world of Troy.

And Stella attended her evening classes regularly during this period. It was then that she began to blossom into a young woman. Her angular movements became softer, and her face rounded out a little. She was now more pretty than beautiful, and pleasing as she was to look at, I'd almost started to prefer her brown clothes.

Then Richard started going out with her. Incidentally, I remember, that happened at my suggestion. I hate engaging in certain discussions, and was glad to have found him a partner. I think he even resisted the idea at first, but I've already mentioned that Richard is very intelligent. The house seamstress sewed Stella a dress from cheap white taffeta, and it made Stella look like a princess from a feature film. Richard was visibly proud and behaved like a benevolent uncle. However, that avuncularity isn't even an act, it's in his nature, alongside some very contrary qualities, and he is very skilled at using it. Richard is a diplomat and a forceful man, so it's hardly a surprise that he's almost always successful. He tries to achieve his goal with the greatest patience and obstinacy—and even in a lovable way. It's only when his charm fails that he begins to get brutal. But not many people know that, and the ones who do have fallen so deeply under his spell that they wouldn't dare to stand up to him.

So off they went to the party, the kindly uncle and the foolish young girl.

Once they'd gone, I went into the kitchen and made dinner for the children, putting everything on a tray and carrying it into the nursery. Annette was lying on the carpet with her legs in the air, reading Mickey Mouse comics. She laughed loudly, and I flinched. Her laughter always gives me a slight shock. I don't understand how an eight-year-old child can laugh like Richard, or rather as Richard would laugh if he were a little girl. Annette is the only one of us who is innocent of Stella's death. Unwittingly, Wolfgang was instrumental in it. It was for his sake, to preserve the illusion that he was growing up in an orderly family, that I tried to keep everything from him. Not only for Wolfgang's sake, however, but also simply out of cowardice and convenience.

Now Wolfgang came out of his room, took the tray with the milk from me and walked with me to the table. There was something touching about this child from his first day onward. He was caring and thoughtful even as a baby, if such a thing is possible.

And even though he doesn't behave very differently from other boys his age, it sometimes seems to me that he acts in this way to fit in with the other boys There are moments when the roles are suddenly reversed and I become a foolish child, while his dark green eyes rest mildly and leniently on me, like a father's eyes. Something very different is concealed beneath his docility and his outward obedience.

Wolfgang is the only person who can make Richard feel uneasy. They also tend to stay out of each other's way, even when they're sitting at the same table.

I put my arm around Wolfgang's shoulders and said, "Wasn't Stella pretty today, just like a princess?" He glared furiously at me. "Like a princess? Ridiculous, she's a silly goose. You're a hundred times more beautiful." I laughed, flattered. "Sweet of you," I said, "but it's not true, and she really did look like a princess." He didn't respond and looked past me.

Later I sat down on the edge of his bed. The light from the streetlight fell on his face. I could see that he was concentrating on something. "What's wrong?" I said, still in a jocular tone. His face, serious and full of concentration a moment before, became soft and childlike in an instant. "Why," he asked, "can't you go away with me in the summer, just with me on my own? Annette can stay with grandma, and Dad is old enough to go off on his own for once."

I thought about it. Wolfgang was right. We could have had a wonderful time together, on a lake somewhere, or in the mountains. Why did I have to go away with Richard every year, when he could have enjoyed himself much more without me? Richard loves speeding in his car, "doing" five cities in a day and then going out in the evening. Every vacation with him uses up the very last of my strength, and it is long into the winter before I've recovered. Every year I dread that trip, and every year I go with him, unable to resist in the end. In fact, why shouldn't I finally be allowed to do what I want—something I've wanted to do for a long time?

"I'll talk to Dad about it," I said. I knew it was difficult. Richard felt obliged to spend his vacation with me. He loathes nothing more than conditions that he describes as slovenly and dissolute, perhaps because that's how he always is himself. In his opinion, it's dissolute and eccentric to use separate bedrooms, not to spend your vacation with your wife, and not to take the children to the zoo or the cinema on Sunday. He would also never separate from me. I am the guardian of his house and his children, and as someone who secretly lives a life of deep anarchy, he values nothing more than outward expressions of order and precision. No one is a stricter guardian of morality than the secret lawbreaker, for it is clear to them that humanity would crumble and perish if everyone lived as they did.

As a very young woman I once asked him, "Why do you love me?" His reply came swiftly and surely: "Because you belong to me."

So he didn't love me because of my looks or my lovable qualities, only as his possession.

He would have loved any random person in my position just as much, and that was the way he loved his children, his house—in short everything that belonged to him. Even then I was beginning to resent this kind of love, but I said nothing, because I'd already learned that any real conversation between us was impossible.

None of his companions will ever make him give up his family—his possessions, that is—and if one day I get the idea into my head that I should leave him, he will stubbornly and vengefully destroy my life. But Richard is one of those men who spoil women's taste in lovers. It would be impossible for me to accept even the quietest of caresses from another man. I am Richard's wife entirely, and since I can no longer bear that, I am condemned to a life of solitude.

For a while all my emotions were concentrated on Wolfgang. I was becoming a crazy mother, and soon recognized the fact myself. Then I started to exert strict control over my behavior. No one knows how often I drew back my already half-raised hand that yearned to touch his hair and his forehead. No one knows how often, standing by the door to the nursery, I turned away in silence and went back to my room. I sealed myself off against the scent of his skin, against his voice and the temptation of his black lashes and rounded cheeks. I allowed myself as much affection as I could, as much as allowed me to live without doing Wolfgang any harm.

But, who knows, perhaps I harm him anyway, perhaps I've always harmed him.

I said, "You've got to go to sleep now, Wolfgang," He put his arms around my neck, pressing his cool nose against my cheek, and said, "And yes, Stella is a silly goose." I pulled gently away from him and left the room. I was sorry that Wolfgang didn't like Stella, because I'd begun to get used to her presence.

Richard and Stella came home late, and I pretended to be asleep, so that a conversation wouldn't leave me wide awake again. Between the narrow slits of my eyelids I saw Richard getting undressed, neatly laying out his clothes—he is very orderly about such matters—and then going to the bathroom. After a while he reappeared, smelling of soap and toothpaste, and moved over to my side. He put his hand below my shoulder and fell asleep on the spot. That movement means: so here I am again, and I hope to find everything in order, that order which happens, in my case, to go by the name of Anna, and sleeps in my bed.

I gave up resisting and pulling away from his hand a long time ago, and this time, once again, I went on calmly lying on it, feeling its warmth through the silk of my nightgown and staring into the darkness. That night I dreamed I had thrown a stone at poor Cassandra in broad daylight, embittered by her prophecies. But the moment I woke up I completely forgot what she'd said to me.

Richard attended another two or three parties with Stella, and she began to move more confidently, speak more freely and become more like people her own age. Even then I couldn't really make conversation with Stella. I sometimes heard her talking to the maid in the kitchen, or playing with Annette, and I was annoyed that I couldn't think of anything to say to her. Wolfgang simply stayed out of her way, and Richard barely seemed to give her any attention at all. He isn't home very much, in fact. Since his office is in the city center, he only comes home for dinner in the evening, and even then it's often very late. I don't know how he spends many of his evenings, and I don't want to.

On Sundays we usually go away with the children, or else Richard goes to the cinema with them, in the last few months with Annette on her own, as Wolfgang is starting to find his own interests and things to do. So he paid no attention to Stella. On Sundays she preferred to stay at home: she darned and washed, manicured her nails, and studied a little. She was probably very bored, as she wasn't a reader. Sometimes I would give her a book. She thanked me, flipped through it a little, and put it back. Her greatest pleasure seemed to be going to the cinema, from which she returned hot and flushed. At the time I often had the impression that Richard was only waiting for the day when this foreign body would vanish from our house again. Then I felt sorry for Stella, but she barely seemed to notice his indifferent attitude.

I never talked to Stella about anything except the most mundane matters. Sometimes I tried to draw her into a conversation, but it didn't elicit even the faintest response. She seemed unable to shed her bashfulness toward me. I attributed this to Luise's bad treatment of her. Every woman Luise's age, every mother, in fact, must have seemed dangerous to Stella.

One March evening Wolfgang and I were sitting at the table. I'd already put Annette to bed. It was very quiet in the room, since neither of us likes listening to music while reading. I thought about how Richard was about to come home and fill our beautiful silence with activity, and the idea made me so uneasy that I couldn't really concentrate on my book. Wolfgang had lowered his face; a dark strand of hair had fallen over his forehead and gleamed red in the lamplight. As always when I watched him reading, I felt a desire to caress him. I didn't, however, because who knows whether he would have liked it. So I settled for passing him a piece of cake, which, with a murmured word of thanks, he set down next to his book. He can't even be bribed with sweets. He accepts them, but then he puts them in his room, until little Annette finds them and eats them.

I'd got to my feet and stepped to the window. It had already been raining for days. And then I saw Stella coming down the garden path, her head lowered, staggering slightly, as if she were drunk or terribly tired.

"Stella's coming," I said, turning around. Wolfgang didn't seem to hear. Stella opened the door and disappeared into the house. I heard her coming up the stairs, opening the door to the apartment, and taking off her coat in the hall. It was five minutes before she came in. Dazzled by the bright light, she closed her eyes.

"You're drenched," I said disapprovingly, "did you forget your umbrella?"

"Yes," Stella said, still breathless, "forgot umbrella." Her hair lay damp and shiny around her head. I poured her some tea, and she joined us at the table and drank in great gulps like someone dying of thirst. "But Stella," I said, "you're shivering, what's wrong?"

She shot me an almost furious look. "Nothing," she said. "Nothing at all, I've just been walking, the streetcar pulled away on me." She crumbled a bread roll, her face turned away.

I suddenly noticed that Wolfgang had stopped reading. He was looking sidelong at Stella through half-lowered eyes, and blushing slowly all the way to his forehead. I followed his gaze and saw that two buttons were missing from her blouse, and her neck looked strangely mottled.

"It's getting late, Wolfgang," I said, "you should go to bed." He stood up without protest and left the room. When he had gone, I wondered whether I should say anything to Stella, but decided not to. She would notice it herself when she got dressed, or else she had already noticed in the hall. She was already so tired that she couldn't sit up straight. She immediately went to bed as well, and I returned to my book. Richard came home in an excellent mood a quarter of an hour later. As clever as he is, there are always lots of details that give him away. When he's cheerful like that, in such a buoyant mood, it means either that he's been drinking or that he's been with a woman. That evening he hadn't been drinking, I could smell from his breath. He had a big appetite and ate more than is healthy for him, in my opinion. As he ate, he told me excitedly about the negotiation he'd been involved in that morning, after which his client had walked free. He wanted to create the impression that this was the reason for his outstanding mood.

But he couldn't fool me, I know his usual cheerful disposition after professional successes, this cheerfulness after evenings out with the boys, and how it differs from his heightened sense of vitality after a dalliance, that triumph of the male who has had his female. Every time Richard tries to mislead me, an incomprehensible feeling of shame falls upon me, even though I'm not the one who should be ashamed. But it is precisely his shamelessness that makes me mute with shame. When that happens I can't look him in the eyes and am unable to respond to the light, conversational tone that he considers appropriate in this case. I am a very bad actress, but then Richard acts for both of us. In the end he stopped talking about it, turned his attention to the newspaper, and drank his red wine with a secret, self-indulgent smile.

I went to bed and pretended to be asleep when he followed me. He considerately turned off the light and pushed his hand under my covers. It settled on my shoulder, and I didn't move. That hand was so warm and vital. Only a few hours before, it had stroked a strange woman, but I wasn't repelled by her. There is nothing repellent about Richard. If I could sweep aside my knowledge of his true nature, nothing would stand in the way of our happiness. And even today I am sometimes filled with a need to forget everything and entrust myself to his big, strong body, the body that's made to take and give pleasure.

Later, the slight pressure of his hand filled me not only with repulsion, but also with a fear that I know only too well. The fear of the superficially tamed predatory beast that, when well fed and looked after, settles for going on little nocturnal raids, after which it comes back to its lair, purring contentedly. And sometimes that animal forgot to erase the traces of its raids in time. Then it would smell of the strange perfume of its victim and wear blood-red lipstick stains on its white shirt collar.

Of course I could have fled, and I toyed with the

idea for years, but in truth it is impossible to leave. Life with Richard has corrupted me and rendered me useless. Anything I started would be pointless, since I know that kind murderers exist. Legal representatives who violate the law every day, bracing cowards and faithful traitors. I had become so familiar with the monstrous mixture of angelic countenance and devil's grimace that any pure, unstained image could only arouse my deepest suspicion.

Richard had fallen asleep. His hand still lay on me, heavy now, unbearably heavy and warm.

I slipped out of bed and went to the kitchen to drink a glass of water.

As I walked past Stella's door I heard her groaning. I stopped and listened. Stella was crying. She wasn't crying discreetly, with restraint, as grown-up people tend to cry, according to the rules of grieving, but rather with wild abandon. It sounded very ugly. The red patches on her neck came to mind. No doubt, Stella was out of control. It would have been my duty to warn her, to scold or talk to her, or at least try to comfort her.

I did none of that. I hate unbridled outbreaks of

emotion, and in any case, it was clear to me that I could no longer hold this girl back once she was roused. She'd been locked for years in a dull, artificial childhood, and all affection had been withheld. The outburst should not have surprised me. I cursed my thoughtlessness, which had led me to give her new clothes and send her out to social gatherings. I knew the men she was likely to meet at these gatherings, none of them better than Richard, but most of them not in his style, revolting, horny little liars. And it would have been an easy matter to seduce a stupid and inexperienced creature like Stella.

I thought about her evening class, and decided to follow her inconspicuously on one occasion, to see who she met.

While I was making this decision, I was well aware that I would never be able to carry out this plan. It was all too pitiful and disgusting.

When I was lying in bed again, it occurred to me that Richard only smelled of his aftershave. The woman he had been with didn't use perfume. I sat up and stared at the face beside me, which was blurring with the pillow, and suddenly I felt ill. I fell back and for a few seconds I felt nothing at all. When I was able to think again, I looked for a sleeping pill in the nightstand and drained my water glass. As so often on nights long forgotten, I had the feeling that something horrific had come so close to my fragile glass wall that I could sense its breath and its stench.

The next morning Stella was pale and her eyelids were red. Richard was leaving a little later than usual, and she asked him to take her a little way in his car. He didn't seem very pleased about the request, but tried not to let his annoyance show and invited Wolfgang to come along as well. I knew he didn't want to be alone with Stella. Even for him, the situation might have been uncomfortable. Wolfgang refused, however; he'd promised to pick up a friend. He spoke to his father very politely, but I sensed the hint of rebelliousness in his voice. Richard raised his eyebrows and seemed to be about to say something, then reconsidered and looked pointedly at his watch.

Only when Annette had finally headed off as well, last of us as usual, did I sit down to breakfast and flip through the newspapers. Then I drew up the menu for the whole week and started watering the flowers.

That always takes a good half hour, we have a lot of flowers standing around, and it's an occupation that grants me the illusion of doing something useful and correct. I'm very well aware, however, that I am squandering my emotions on things that don't need them. Stella's sobbing in the night hadn't moved me at all, it had only revolted and confused me. The fact that the young cactus had died was a real worry to me.

I love flowers even more than animals, because they are mute, they can't jump around or disturb me in my fruitless, manic thoughts.

The help came and busied herself in the kitchen. I stood by the window in the sitting room, the little watering can in my hand, staring out into the garden. The morning wind rustled in the bushes, which are still quite bare, and it seemed to me that this constant trembling of the branches, this quiet, secret unease, was trying to say something to me, something that I couldn't understand but was clearly very important. I remembered certain days of my childhood that were without grief and melancholy, without even sympathy. The little girl from back then was dead, strangled and beaten by big, skillful hands. It wasn't anything to be sorry about, because she had barely defended herself, and you don't need to grieve for things and people that don't defend themselves.

At last the woman came into the room, and I went next door and looked out into the garden from there.

The mailman came. I heard the mail falling through the mailbox, but didn't move. I don't expect mail—I never expect letters. The only person who could write me an important letter is me, so it will never be written. I heard the girl carrying the mail into the sitting room, and went on staring into the confusion of the branches. The buds on the trees and bushes had plumped up a little after the rain, and the young grass glistened with moisture.

In the old days I sometimes yielded to temptation and went down into the garden, but it had always been a disappointment to me. Here, from the window, it's exactly the right distance for me.

So I stood at the window and knew that I had to call Richard. I could already hear his surprised, protesting voice. He never admits to anything, this is all part of his tactics. And that is his strength, because it means that credulous people have absolute trust in him, and suspicious ones bounce off the smooth wall of his denial. If he did care about Stella, that is, as long as her healthy young body still attracted him, he wouldn't give her up, but once his passion expired, nothing would be able to keep him from dropping her. And I also knew that she was utterly devoted and enslaved to him, and would rather let herself be killed than betray him.

I gazed into the seething mass of the budding branches and thought about the short time left for Stella's happiness, and it suddenly seemed pointless to destroy even that brief span by intervening.

In fact there was no longer anything that could done. Stella would suffer violently for a while, and then start to calm down, as we must all calm down if we want to stay alive. She would marry one of those men that one marries after a disappointment, and have children and slowly learn to forget. But she would never again be the person she had been before she came to our house and aroused Richard's desire.

I hated and feared confrontations with Richard. He is vengeful and cruel in the punishments he dreams up for me. All of those punishments involve

Wolfgang. He is devilishly clever, and it scares me. Of course I knew this was an unworthy thought. My peace and comfort, even Wolfgang's peace, both were unimportant compared to a helpless young person being ruined in front of my eyes for the sake of a pleasure that Richard could have had from any streetwalker.

I closed the window and knew that I wouldn't talk to Richard.

Springtime came. Stella had calmed down again, and was completely filled with her secret happiness. She now looked like a young woman, and that made her more ordinary than she had been before. She often retreated to her room. No one missed her, incidentally, apart from little Annette, who sometimes knocked in vain at her door before finally turning to other games.

Wolfgang continued to avoid her, and Richard had never given her a thought anyway. He barely saw her at home, almost only on Sundays. He was agonizingly restless during those weeks, he always came home late, and his constant cheerfulness was beginning to get on my nerves. He's the type of person who fills a room with their vital force, to the point that you think you will suffocate in their vicinity.

Annette was the only one who didn't sense this. His proximity to her cranked her liveliness up into boisterousness, and the delight that Richard took in her could not be ignored. She can get him to do whatever she wants, and exploits the fact with brazen displays of affection, every inch his daughter in this respect as well. On the other hand, Richard was starting to find Wolfgang weird, with his quiet politeness, which assumed a degree of arrogance next to Richard's joviality.

Wolfgang was standing by the window looking into the garden. When he heard me, he turned around and I saw that his eyes were quite dark, with rage, worry, or even just reflection. But he immediately gave me his shy smile, which was intended to mislead me about his state of mind.

"What are you thinking about?" I asked.

"As it happens, mother," he said, "I was thinking that the tiniest dog or even a bee is of much greater value than anything else, I mean, a cathedral, for example, or an airplane."

I stared at him, filled with admiration and delight. Was it not incredible that this thought, which I'd never spoken out loud, had grown in his brain? It made me feel both proud and happy, but he was already mitigating his words. "Perhaps that's not quite true either, though, because you basically get a dog for free, don't you?" Something about this fact struck him as not quite right, because it really isn't quite right. I could see the doubt at work behind his eyes; his confusion was obvious. I quickly said, "You're absolutely correct, things don't just have a financial value, they also have a natural value that remains unchanged for thousands of years. Everything else is nothing, all that really counts is life." I didn't feel entirely comfortable saying these words, and wished he could have continued living for a while without them, untroubled and free of doubts.

Very soon, I knew, he too would begin to suffer. Perhaps I'm too fond of this child, because for countless days and nights during the war I carried him into the basement, hugging him tightly, to give him the warmth he needed, with no thought but that of saving this little seed of life. At the time I also believed in love and in Richard, which meant one and the same thing to me. But I still had Wolfgang, and in my dreams I'm carrying that little bundle in dark basements, through the dust and the burning smell of collapsing buildings.

How easy, on the other hand, everything had been with Annette, the birth in a clean and quiet clinic, the well-fed suckling, all so effortless, almost casual, like acquiring a little cat that started crawling through the rooms and was soon standing on its own feet. Annette might as well have been the child of an acquaintance who happened to be visiting, a child that one feeds and bathes, whose hair one combs, on whose feet one puts little white socks, and from whose healthy young scent one quietly warms oneself.

Annette had never been a problem, and she never would be. The quiet unease that sometimes creeps over me when she's nearby, when she climbs into my lap and kisses me, is does not apply to her, and I dismiss these feelings as soon as they arise.

It's pleasant being kissed by Annette, even though I know that she kisses her father, the lady from the dairy, the doctor and neighbor's dog just as passionately as she sometimes kisses me. Her kisses are only a sudden surge and don't mean anything, they are perfectly noncommittal and forgotten a moment later.

Wolfgang doesn't kiss anyone. If he presses his nose to my cheek for a moment, it's incredibly significant to me, especially compared to Annette's kisses.

Now he had turned back toward the window, and for some reason I thought it appropriate to draw his thoughts to something else.

"Wouldn't you like to go and see Fritz," I said, "or Aunt Ella?" But he didn't want to. I became distinctly aware that I was starting to bother him, so I left, and he stayed by the window, motionless.

After a quarter of an hour I found him with that same attitude, and I didn't like it. "We could go and see a documentary at the cinema," I suggested, "and then pick up Dad from the office."

He turned around sharply. "No," he said, "let's not go to Dad's. But we could go for a walk, window shopping and so on." I didn't care either way. Aware that I was fulfilling an important duty, I put on my coat and hat. I couldn't understand why Wolfgang, who had told me yesterday day how much he wanted to see the film, now all of a sudden wanted to look at shop window displays, when the weather was so harsh and windy—but perhaps the fresh air would do us both good. We wandered the streets for an hour, and Wolfgang became feverishly cheerful, drawing my attention to this and that, and playacting so obviously that my heart grew quite heavy with concern. Something about him wasn't right. My head was buzzing when we got home, and Wolfgang sat down at the table and changed very suddenly from one minute to the next. Pale, and with dark circles around his eyes, he sat hunched over his cocoa and looked sad beyond expression. I put him to bed myself and waited until he had gone to sleep. Then I remembered that spring is always exhausting and uncomfortable, a time that takes its toll on him.

I was tired too, and didn't wait for Richard. Annette was at her grandmother's, so I was able to lie down. I didn't hear Richard coming in, and also I didn't see Stella until breakfast.

The incident with the violets happened on one of the following days. I remember exactly, it was a Wednesday, one of the days when Stella didn't attend her Italian class. She was suddenly standing in front of me in the room, wearing that slightly too-tight black dress of hers, and holding a little bouquet of violets out to me. "The flowers are fabulously beautiful," I said, taking them from her. I felt sorry for her. I had an idea of what she must have been going through. Her expression was oppressed and pleading, and all of a sudden I saw her once again as the big, clumsy child that she was when she first came to us. I leaned forward a little and kissed her on the cheek. She recoiled in horror, and it seemed for a moment that she was about to throw herself sobbing around my neck. An uncontrolled movement on my part—I had instinctively taken a step back—snapped her out of it. And nothing happened. Stella went to her room and I returned to mine, and then I dismissed her from my mind, as I had been doing for weeks.

A little later Wolfgang asked me who had brought the violets. At the sound of Stella's name he suddenly looked angry and embittered, like a very old man, and immediately he walked away.

And later, as I lay reading, I forgot Stella, the violets, and myself. But I didn't forget Wolfgang; he was constantly present, a troubling unease, just below the threshold of my consciousness.

April came. I did my tasks as always, the housework continued without a hitch. Annette brought bad grades home, and I gave her a dictation every day. Wolfgang was spending most of his time at a friend's house, and I can't actually remember Richard, he must have been as he always was. Nothing extraordinary happened to him either. He was bringing an affair to an end, a process that he had experienced so often that it couldn't have knocked him off-balance.

Stella's classes had finished, for no apparent reason, in the middle of the year. She no longer even tried to lie to me, and I didn't ask. I was careful to spare her, and stop torturing her further with pointless questions. Now she spent every evening at home, and I often sat with her over a cup of tea, waiting for Richard. But he was overwhelmed with work and always came home late. Sometimes he came home smelling of an unfamiliar perfume, and I hoped Stella wouldn't notice. On this particular evening, I wished she had already gone to bed, but she went on sitting there reading the paper, even though she was so tired that she could barely keep her eyes open.

She wasn't reading the paper, however, she was just sitting motionless, holding it up in front of her eyes. She had completely forgotten that when you're reading the paper you have to turn the page from time to time. I knew what was going on in her mind. Wild with longing and despair, she was waiting at least to see Richard, to hear his voice and catch a glance from him. I could imagine the humiliations that she had already endured, and the ones still ahead of her. And I wondered a hundred times whether or not I should speak to her. I didn't want to hear a confession, because there was nothing I could have said in response, and I was fed up with lying.

That evening—Richard had finally come home—I went into the kitchen again to make fresh tea. When I came back and stood outside the door, I heard Richard talking to Stella. Our doors shut very tightly, and I couldn't make out a word, but the bitterly cold and angry tone of his voice didn't escape me. Stella must have been particularly stubborn, because it isn't Richard's style to speak to a woman like that. I tapped the door with the tea tray, and finally walked into the room with an indifferent smile on my lips.

Stella was leaning against the oven, crumpling a handkerchief in her hand. Her face was as white as the wall and I looked away immediately.

She said "good night" in a voice that made me shiver, and left the room on quick, blind steps.

"Stella looks miserable," I said. Richard shrugged. "Who knows who she's hanging around with," he said. "I'll be glad when she's back and happy with her mother. The responsibility is too much for us. We don't have time to keep a proper eye on her."

I said nothing. How could I have responded? The lamplight rested on his blooming, smooth face, and when I bent down to pour the tea, I caught a strange and delicate scent. Then when I was sat across from him, studying his completely peaceful and indifferent expression and thinking about Stella, who might have been lying on her bed sobbing at that moment, I felt a wave of nausea and vertigo. "It isn't possible," I thought, "it just can't be so." But I knew it was possible and that I'm just incapable of comprehending it.

It was very late when we finally went to bed.

The next day Stella came home from school at four o'clock and immediately went to her room. When she didn't appear for dinner, I brought her a tray of tea and sandwiches. She was deathly pale, her lips were sore and strangely red, and seemed to be swollen. She said something about a splitting headache and turned to face the wall. I gave her a powder and left her alone. She spent the whole of the next day in bed, she didn't eat anything and kept her face turned toward the wall. She didn't have a fever, and her pulse was normal. When she got up again and went to school she'd changed completely. She barely came to the living room now, she spent lots of time lying on her bed, sometimes looking at me like a lunatic. And again I didn't ask, afraid of what I would hear. I was still of the ludicrous opinion that I was able to keep myself—and therefore Wolfgang too—out of Richard's dark machinations. I felt genuine concern at the sight of her beautiful face, captive to a wild, mute pain, but I didn't want to break through the wall that still separated me from that pain.

One afternoon I invited her to go into town with me, hoping to being able to distract her a little. We did a few errands. Stella quite absent in her new state of madness; I was hesitant, clumsy, and somewhat repelled. I noticed that people were staring at us, and I finally took Stella to a café where Richard sometimes meets his chess acquaintances. I felt terrible and awkward next to this sleepwalking goddess of misfortune, and really felt like slapping her awake from her trance.

"Stella," I said sharply. "Stella." She didn't hear me. She looked past me, her eyes wide with horror. I followed her gaze and saw that someone was waving at me from the next table. It was an acquaintance of Richard's, a certain Dr. W., a gynecologist whose practice isn't far from Richard's office. Richard once represented him in a divorce case, and represented him well. This Dr. W. wanted to get rid of his wife, and arranged circumstances so that one of his friends was caught with her. It's an old trick, of course, and everyone knew how it was done and they were all highly amused by it. But he had a guilt-free divorce and didn't have to pay alimony.

I feel ill whenever I see this person.

Stella was now gazing convulsively into her cup. I paid and said, "Let's go, Stella." She nodded and got to her feet. When we were in the street, I linked arms with her and felt her trembling.

What was going to become of this big unhappy child by my side? Rage and shame drove the blood into my heart. But I said nothing. Once we were home I immediately sent Stella to bed and gave her one of my sleeping powders. She looked gratefully up at me and pressed her face against my hand. I quickly pulled my hand away. Now, Stella really had no reason to be grateful to me.

Richard came home in an excellent mood. His eyes were blue, moist, and excited. He kissed me on the cheek, and I was surprised not to feel revulsion.

"What have you been doing all day?" he asked me cheerfully. "I was in town with Stella," I said. "Incidentally, we bumped into your friend Dr. W."

Silence. Then he said, his voice with a hint of cautious suspicion, "Friend is overstating it, I haven't seen him for an eternity. No other news?"

"Nothing else," I said, looking at him. I'm unlucky enough for people to be able to read my eyes. Richard must have been startled by what he read in mine, and he really was.

He immediately looked away from me and said in a calm and pleasant voice, the voice of a man of honor: "And what has Wolfgang been doing all this time, I hope there's nothing to complain about."

"No," I said, "nothing to complain about." I could have laughed in his face. I wanted to say to him, "My dear husband, you don't need to remind me that you can't blackmail me with Wolfgang. I already know how exposed I am to you." But I didn't say it. He would punish me ruthlessly, punish both me and Wolfgang, who was completely innocent. Stella was not my child. And she was beyond help. I had no way of helping her now. I knew she would soon go back to the small town where she was from, and I wouldn't have to see her ever, ever again.

Nauseous and suddenly very tired, I went to bed. A little later I felt Richard's hand on my shoulder and smelled his clean breath. He told me about a ring he had seen, which would go wonderfully with my evening dress. I didn't move, but he didn't draw his hand back, so we lay there until we'd gone to sleep. That night I dreamed I was trapped in a basement. A huge pile of charred masonry lay on top me, gradually crushing me.

The next week passed relatively quickly. The painters came to the house and painted all the window frames. That gave Richard an excuse to start coming home only to sleep, and I was grateful to him for his absence. It was also better for Stella not to see him for a while.

That week in particular was very cool and rainy, and the draught from our window frames made us shiver pitifully. Unease and damp filled the house from basement to loft. I was constantly chasing after Annette to keep her away from the sticky doors and windows, but she still ended up with broad white stripes on her green velvet dress, which neither turpentine nor any other cleaner could get rid of.

Stains are a strange thing in general. Never in my life have I managed to get rid of one completely. I have a deep suspicion of women who claim to be able to remove stains. Either they're lying or there's something not quite right at home. At any rate our clothes make their way to the dry cleaners, from which I get them back clean, admittedly, but turned into transparent little rags. They probably use razor blades and sandpaper to remove stains. Annette's green skirt was one of those lost, and even after coming back from the cleaner it will barely be any use to anyone.

But after everything else that has happened, it really doesn't matter. Annette got a slap and sat stubborn and weeping on the woodbox in the kitchen, her petticoat pulled over her knees. At last Wolfgang took pity and took her for a walk. That happened on the first day of this disaster. The days that followed were no different.

In the end, when we were all sighing with relief, it turned out that the painter had switched the windows around and it was impossible to close any of them. Wolfgang and I worked for half a day to sort it out and fell exhausted into bed in the evening.

Throughout this entire time, Stella paid no attention to us. In the morning she went to school as before, and in the afternoon she lay on her bed and stared at the wall.

My work, as tedious and unpleasant as I found it, suited me well enough. It simply made it impossible for me to deal with Stella. I understood her situation very well, but I couldn't imagine what needed to happen now, and I was least of all able to expect help in the matter from Richard. As far as he was concerned, Stella wasn't there. He'd sorted out everything that he could, and went about his business wearing the face of an overstretched man who must on no account be disturbed in his important work.

On Sunday we drove the car—it had finally stopped raining—into the countryside. Stella turned down my invitation, using the excuse that she had to do her homework. I was glad not to see her for the day. Sitting next to Richard in the car, I relaxed a little and completely forgot about her for several hours. Richard was enchantingly merry and visibly determined to make the day as pleasant for me as possible. No one can do that as well as he can, and not even the thought that he was doing it for a very particular purpose could seriously bother me, weary and exhausted as I was. We were a happy family, and I refused to notice that Wolfgang was being very quiet in the back seat, and not responding to Annette's chatter as he usually did.

In the evening I didn't go into Stella's room as usual. I thought she could at least have come into the kitchen to say hello to me. The idea of having to look at her again every day made me quite weak with irritation and impatience.

I began to understand Richard, who so ruthlessly avoids engaging with ill and unhappy people.

On Monday morning, just after I'd finished my breakfast, the phone rang. I reluctantly tore myself away from the view of the pale blue sky above the top of the linden tree and went into the hall.

At first I couldn't understand a thing, but the strange man's voice repeated everything to me very precisely, clearly, and slowly. I got dressed and drove to the emergency room. While they were operating on Stella, I sat and waited in a little room for visitors. They had hardly allowed me any hope; she was not expected to regain consciousness. I stared at the pattern in the floor and tried to shake off my agonizing stiffness.

An African hemp plant stood on a little table, and I started counting its bright, heart-shaped leaves. Stella, I thought, six, seven, eight and again Stella.

The little tree tottered and leaned toward me, then the floor rushed up at me.

Someone wiped my painful face. "You should have your heart looked at," the nurse said. I laughed loudly. She looked at me severely and stuck a needle in my arm. "There's nothing to laugh about," she said. I fell into a shocked silence— I had no idea that I'd been laughing. My heart was in fine condition, it was even strong and powerful, no one knew that better than me. I sat up and asked about Stella. The nurse didn't know anything yet, she was from the ambulance service and had nothing to do with the emergency room.

"Is she your daughter?" she asked, relenting a little, and obviously inclined to forgive my inappropriate laughter.

I said "No," and she seemed to regret her softness immediately. "Lie back," she ordered angrily, "and remember that these things happen for our own good, even if we don't understand." I obeyed. The nurse was certainly right, and even if she hadn't been, I was in no position to argue. She had unbuttoned the collar of my blouse, and when she looked away I quickly did it up again. That action also brought back my strength and composure. "I'm feeling better already," I dared to say. She looked at me doubtfully and then left me with the threat that she would shortly come and check up on me. I sat up and waited.

When the doctor came, I could already tell from the expression on his face that Stella was dead. They had only operated as a formality. In fact I had expected nothing less, impressed as I was by the thoroughness with which they went about things. "Do you want me to call a taxi?" said the tall, strange man in the white coat. I nodded, and he gave the task to a nurse. He also said that it would be better if I didn't look at her, given my weakened state. But I insisted, and he brought me to her with a shrug.

The notion that this strange white bundle was supposed to be Stella, who had been alive when she left me two hours earlier, was impossible to grasp I laid my hand on her cheek, which was already quite cool, even colder than my hand. Then the car was there. I was handed Stella's bag and went home.

Now I really should have called Richard, but a dark feeling of shame prevented me. Not because I thought I needed to spare him, but because it seemed like a crime against Stella to talk to Richard about her.

Three or four times I went into the hall, picked up the receiver, and set it back down again. In the end I found myself standing by the window, smoking, my mind completely blank, staring into the garden.

After the week of rain, a radiantly beautiful day had broken. Drops of water quivered on the young linden leaves, and the air streamed through the window, fresh and clean.

Stella was dead, and I felt a great sense of relief. Never again would I have to rack my brains for something to say to her, never again would I see her pale, shattered face. Stella was dead, and I could return to my old life with Wolfgang, the garden, and the good order of everyday life. The relief was so great that I started laughing softly.

Wolfgang came home at around midday. I told him what had happened, and he asked, rather untroubled, I thought: "Does Dad know?" Later he went into the hall and made a phone call. I heard him saying, "Stella is dead, Dad. Yes, I'm staying at home. Maybe you could come home earlier. At the emergency room, yes, good." Suddenly I started shivering; the person talking out there was not mine, my child that I had pressed to my heart, dragged through the days of bombing, but a strange, embittered man, completely grown-up, cold, and pitiless.

I heard him going into the kitchen and busying himself with the tea things. I obediently drank the hot tea that he brought me. I had a desire to set down the cup, draw Wolfgang to me and weep at last, but I felt ashamed in the presence this new Wolfgang, who sat beside me so severely, so stiffly upright, not even looking at me. It was only when he had pulled a blanket over me and left the room that I turned toward the wall and began to weep. I wept for Wolfgang, for Stella, for Richard, and for me, and I felt as if I might never stop weeping. I felt the damp on my cheeks and on my hands and tasted the saltiness of tears in my mouth. I slowly became dull, empty, and peaceful.

Richard came home toward evening. He had been to the hospital already, and had sorted everything out with the head of the department, whom he knew well. I didn't ask him whether he had seen Stella, probably not. For the first time I was glad that I didn't have to be alone with Wolfgang anymore.

He left immediately, incidentally, when his father came to bring Annette home from her grandmother's, where he had sent her at midday.

Richard came and sat with me and gave me a cigarette. I saw that he was irritated with Stella's inappropriate behavior. She had always done what he demanded of her, and now, when he had thought everything had been operating most efficiently, she had to go and cause trouble for him. "It was an accident," he said, "an accident, without question."

I just nodded and said nothing. The warmth of his hand passed through my dress and filled me with peace and comfort. My brain knew who Richard was, but my miserable, weakened body greedily absorbed the warmth and stability that emanated from him.

I went to sleep right away.

The next day I resumed my activity. After the funeral and after Luise's hasty departure, it sometimes felt for hours at a time as if Stella had never come to our house. Luise had taken her daughter's things with her, the spare room was empty, and the bed was freshly made. Not a trace of Stella.

I'm beginning to get tired. I've been writing for two days. Soon Richard will come home with Annette and Wolfgang will arrive a little later. I don't know what is going to happen to us. I don't know. I would like to close my eyes, sleep and forget, but I can't do it. I will open the window and let air into the room. Over the past few hours I have forgotten about the bird in the linden tree. It's no longer sitting on its branch. Its mother didn't come. Its little belly is probably lying somewhere down in the shrubbery; in a few days it will have disappeared, broken, as if it had never existed. I wish its mother had found it and brought it to safety, but I never really believed that would happen.

Now I'm hoping for a miracle, for the little bird to be sitting warm and safe in the nest, for Stella to step into the room in her cheerful red dress, young, lively, and still untouched by death and love, and for Wolfgang to press his face against mine again, making my heart quiver with tenderness. And I wish I could lie in Richard's arms, without fear and dread, yield utterly to the soothing warmth of his big body.

And then I wake from my fantasies, and the knowledge assails me like a blow to my chest.

Nothing can erase the day when Wolfgang said, with his back to me, "Can you inform Dad that in the autumn I would like to go to a boarding school in the country?"

I stared at the small and independent nape beneath the shining dark hair.

"But," I stammered, "but Wolfgang, why?"

He ignored my question, as a well-mannered person ignores inappropriate questions.

"It's too late to apply," I said hastily, "we should have done that before."

Suddenly he turned to me. "I wrote to them myself, Mom. You've always said that city air isn't good for me. They still have free spaces. I think Dad will be all right with it."

Oh yes, and how all right he will be, I thought bitterly. There it was again, that feeling of shame toward the boy who had been my child. I breathed deeply and said, "Perhaps you're right. Dad will come round in the end. Your health really isn't the best. And then in the holidays," I added, "it will be that much lovelier."

He lowered his long eyelashes and said: "Of course, Mom." Then he came to me and pressed his cheek to mine for a moment. The cool, revolted knowledge in his eyes was dimmed by a hint of sympathy and grief.

But I don't like pity. "It's fine," I said, "I'll talk to Dad."

He went out the door and I stayed back alone, for ever and ever.

I suddenly had the idea of packing my suitcase and leaving with Wolfgang. I could rent two rooms in another city, for me and the children, and start all over again.

But of course I knew that was impossible.

At one point everything was fine and orderly, and then someone muddled the threads. I can no longer find the beginning, and the weave under my hands becomes more confused by the day, it grows and burgeons, and one day it will bury and suffocate me.

I'm frightened. Every day I pull myself a hundred times from a trance and say to myself: Stop thinking, walk away from the window, abandon your pitiful habits, staring into the garden like this and walking from one room to the other. There's nothing for you to see in the garden.

Take care of the house, look after Annette, and think of your duties.

Then I pick up my bag and go shopping, but something leaps out at me in the shop, from the eyes of the dead fishes and the pale pink flesh of the slaughtered calves, and I run from them, and as I walk down the street I feel their staring eyes on my back. But I don't look back, because it isn't worth looking back. Exhausted and trembling, I sit down again on the sofa and my thoughts start running away, and everything starts all over again. Luise comes into the room and asks me if I could take in Stella for a school year, and I don't dare to say no, don't dare say no to her angry little ferrety face. I set the lace doily back down on the chest of drawers and put the greyhounds on it, the horses and the dancers, and we collect Stella from the station, a little gloomy about the disturbance that she will mean for us. Richard barely wastes a glance on her, he sometimes smells of Chanel No. 4, and Stella isn't yet in danger. She sits hunched over her exercise books in her brown clothes and gets bored or knits socks for the poor.

"We should buy her some clothes, and she'd be a beauty," I say to Richard, and then comes the day when he sees Stella for the first time.

Yes, I know how it all happened. I rewound the reel, and now I can see that this was what had to happen. I experience the evenings with Wolfgang again, we talk about Achilles and Cassandra, and I'm happy.

Of course I could also think about the future, but I never do that. It will come without any intervention from me and in some strange way the future will turn us into something that we never wanted to be. Every minute, every second transforms us further from ourselves.

And I fear nothing more than the day when I will forget that everything was once different. I try to recall to myself the feeling that I had after going to bed, that vibrant silence, the slow sinking into sleep, still without fear and regret, and awaking in the gloom, alone, blissful, and at one with myself. When will I forget the tenderness that swept over me as I held Wolfgang in my arms?

I hear footsteps on the gravel path, Richard's tread and Annette's hurrying little steps. Without going to the window I can see him walking slowly so she doesn't get tired out, his hand surrounding her round child's hand, and I see him patiently answering her questions.

For a heartbeat I am transformed into the little girl, in a world of sweet, cheerful warmth, holding hands with a kind and almighty father.

And while Stella's flesh comes away from her bones and drenches the planks of the coffin, the face of her murderer is reflected in the blue sky of an innocent child's eyes.